Marketing Your Busir

A practical step-by-ste
business owners and

Internet Handbooks

Other titles in preparation

Marketing
Your Business
on the internet

A practical step-by-step guide for all
business owners and managers

Sara Edlington

Second edition

www.internet-handbooks.co.uk

Published by Internet Handbooks, a Division of International Briefings Ltd,
Plymbridge House, Estover Road, Plymouth PL6 7PY, United Kingdom.

Telephone (Customer Services)	(01752) 202301
Fax (Customer Services)	(01752) 202331
Email (Customer Services)	cservs@plymbridge.com
Email (Editorial)	publisher@internet-handbooks.co.uk
Distributor's web site	http://www.plymbridge.com
Publisher's web site	http://www.internet-handbooks.co.uk

Typeset by PDQ Typesetting, Newcastle-under-Lyme.

Printed and bound by The Cromwell Press Ltd, Trowbridge, Wiltshire.

Contents

Contents...

List of illustrations

Preface to the Second Edition

. . . .

This book was first written as a result of conversations with many business people who wanted to use practical, tried and tested methods to market their company online, but could not find a ready source of manageable information. The internet marketing approaches and techniques discussed here have been applied very successfully by myself, by my clients, by people I have encountered at conferences, and by successful online companies in the UK and elsewhere.

According to certain pundits, online marketing is a complex technical science that few business people are capable of understanding. Ordinary business managers and entrepreneurs are supposed to stand passively by while others call the shots. This is not the case. It is true that marketing a business in this strange new electronic environment does call for some challenging new ways of thinking. More and more people are beginning to realise that the internet is set to be the most important new marketing environment of our age. Everyone responsible for a commercial activity now needs to take full account of it.

The rise and – at the time of writing – the fall of some of the so-called dot coms has frightened off many businesses from going online. Many others, and you may be among them, are disillusioned by the prospect of spending time and money on a web site that appears unable to pay its way.

When this book first appeared, I received an email from a gentleman attacking my 'old economy/old marketing' ideas. He believed that with the coming of the internet, the old economy went out of the window. I recently wrote back to the person in question and directed him towards the web site of a small, family-owned business. This family runs a small agricultural manufacturing business. It would appear to be a dying business sector – manufacturing – in a market which is in deep depression, farming. The firm's director, and his mother, were sceptical that a web site would be able to sell machinery costing thousands of pounds.

It did, it has done, and continues to do so. In fact, the web site has paid for itself many times over. The business is marketed using a combination of some of the techniques discussed in this book, and a regular small ad in *Farmer's Weekly*. You can visit that site at www.edlington.com – and yes, the firm belongs to part of my family, and I designed and marketed the site. It is a case study of the new economy being mixed with the old.

The book is intended to guide you step by step through the process of getting your company successfully online, through the various stages of electronic marketing, and finally to the forefront of this extraordinary new flattened and borderless world of cyberspace. You should be able to achieve what my family's firm, and many others, have achieved, and be ready both to survive and prosper in this fast-changing world.

The jargon in the book has been kept to a minimum, so you can quickly absorb everything, give it due consideration, and start successfully marketing your own enterprise in this burgeoning online world.

The book's web site will be regularly updated with more tried and tested marketing methods you can use, together with details of the latest business trends you can benefit from. The internet is the most amazing phenomenon of our times, and we are lucky to be at the forefront of what will surely by an economic and social revolution almost without parallel. It offers a huge opportunity for even the smallest business to take its products or services to global market at minimal cost. So seize the hour – and go for it!

I would like to thank the following people for their inspiration and support: my late father who sadly didn't live to see this book published; my mother, for being a limitless source of help through some difficult times; Bruce Tober and Neil Barrick; Bruce Davidson, for supporting me through the early stage of my writing career; my daughter Elizabeth, for disturbing me at all the right moments; and finally, my cats, for disturbing me when Libby couldn't.

Sara Edlington

saraedlington@internet-handbooks.co.uk

1 Throw out the rule book!

In this chapter we will explore:

▶ *doing business in the age of the internet*
▶ *ten reasons why internet marketing is very different from real-world marketing*
▶ *how internet marketing works*
▶ *why your business can be an internet marketing success*
▶ *how much it will cost you to create a web site to market your company.*

. . . .

Doing business in the age of the internet

Marketing on the internet is a paradox. Many aspects of it are similar to traditional marketing, such as knowing your market and targeting your marketing materials to that market. But other aspects of marketing on the internet are completely different. Be ready to lay aside all your preconceptions, and be prepared to bring a completely open mind to this challenging new business environment.

The advent of the internet and the age of digitalised information represents one of the biggest revolutions which has taken place in modern history – and this revolution is only now just beginning. Almost no individual, no company, and no private or public organisation on the planet will remain unaffected by it. All the rules of business are changing. Information can traverse the planet at almost the speed of light. With this amazing new technology, transactions can cross every traditional boundary – of geography and location, of language, of national culture, of politics, of bureaucracy and regulation. We are rapidly entering a new 'borderless world' of electronic commerce. The new markets will be global, and the opportunities vast – but while offering huge rewards for the adventurous and imaginative, this new marketplace will also be competitive as never before, as customers click their way in seconds from web site to web site across the ever-expanding internet.

Ten reasons why internet marketing is different

There are ten reasons why internet marketing is different from marketing in the 'real-world'.

1. Customers expect to be able to get in touch with you 24 hours a day.
2. The internet is a so-called 'multi-phased' medium. That is, you can use it as a direct selling tool, as a way of generating sales leads, as a means to provide customer support, or as a brand-building tool. Or all of them!
3. The internet is interactive in a way that traditional marketing materials aren't. The more interactive your web site is, the more your customers

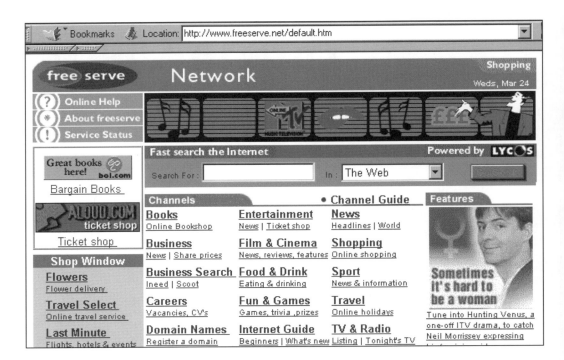

Fig. 1. Freeserve has led the way in free internet service provision in the UK. Owned by Dixons and PC World, it has shot up in the popularity stakes, and brought more than a million prospective new UK customers online.

and clients will use it.

4. The internet is a 'pull-me' rather than 'push-you' technology. Both of these are marketing terms, probably devised by someone who liked Dr Doolittle. A 'push-you' technology is a sales letter or similar. They're items that come to you. A 'pull-me' technology is one where the customer or client seeks you out.

5. The internet is constantly growing and changing. New technologies arrive almost weekly, making it vital that you keep up with them and preferably ahead of them. A new technology could harm your online marketing, or it could help your marketing enormously.

6. Your marketing has to keep changing. Whereas you may use a successful sales letter for several years, the content of web sites has to change at least monthly, otherwise it's considered old and not worth reading.

7. Finding and exploiting a niche is more important online than offline. And just to confuse matters more, a niche online can be far more focused than one offline.

8. Mass marketing doesn't work well. The big companies who are on the internet such as the search engines Yahoo! and Excite! are good examples of this. They are trying to use mass marketing techniques to make money. So far the results are patchy at best. The secret to success is reason no. 7 above.

9. Customers and clients are more demanding. They expect to be entertained, informed, kept ahead of their rivals, and treated as if you knew them personally. They are also notoriously fickle, but are extremely loyal to sites they like.

10. If the above has made you feel like running to cancel your internet account, then consider this. The internet allows you to access customers across the globe, at any time of the day or night. Your web site is working 24 hours a day, seven days a week, all year for you. It doesn't want coffee breaks, holidays or a company car. The internet is one of the most powerful marketing mediums to arrive since advertising and direct mail were invented. And it could make your company a lot of money – perhaps even a fortune.

Questions and answers

You say that internet marketing and 'real-world' marketing are different but in many ways the same. What do you mean by this?

The internet is another marketing technology, like sales letters, direct mail, ads and so on. They are in effect the same, they market your company, yet different, in that an ad is a short piece of marketing communication which is only used in magazines and newspapers. But an ad is still a marketing communication, just like a direct mail letter is. A sales letter would look out of place in a newspaper, and an ad would look a bit odd if you sent it straight to the customer.

This is what we mean by the internet being the same, but different. The internet has many unique features which make it different from the sales letter, just as the sales letter has unique features that the ad doesn't have. People react differently to each, and it's the same with the internet. If you're worried that you haven't the resources to market your company online, think again. Even the smallest company of just one person can market their company effectively online.

But does internet marketing work?

In a word, yes. But since you're a businessperson who has no doubt visited the school of hard knocks, that isn't going to be enough. Here are some examples of businesses, drawn from personal experience.

The reproduction antiques manufacturer

This particular company employs four people and manufactures repro duction antiques. These reproductions are so good that it is difficult to tell them from the real thing. The firm has a loyal customer base amongst large companies who want antiques but can't afford the insurance for the real thing, and home owners who love antiques, but hate the price tags.

The company spent £2,500 getting a site designed and the content written. The cost included having it placed on all the major search engines, and on other smaller ones that fitted their market profile. The site contained photographs of their goods, ordering information, a regular column about antiques, some of the interesting stories behind the real antiques, and a special calculator that lets you see what reproductions you can afford within your budget. The site was then marketed using the techniques you'll read about in this book. Within a week, they had received 15 orders from abroad and four new orders from their existing customers. Since then the site has made them a consistent £25,000 in sales for the two years it has been running. It could make a lot more, but the company does not have the time to market it as much as they would like. It is therefore about to ask an internet marketing agent to market it for them.

The blind-maker

This firm employs 50 people. They make blinds for office windows. You name it, and they can make it. When they sought professional advice, their market was becoming very competitive and they were worried that they would have to let some of their people go if things did not pick up soon. The company spent £1,500 on site design, content, and search engine placement. On their site are samples of the patterns for the blinds you can buy, information about maintaining the blinds and solving common problems, such as stuck tracks, ordering and delivery information, and a colour chart so that you can be certain your chosen blind fits in with your office décor.

Again, the site was marketed using the ideas and techniques in this book. At first nothing much seemed to happen and the company began to get nervous. But they decided to carry on marketing the web site, as they realised that a site sitting there gathering dust does not generate any sales. Two weeks later, they received four orders, and a week later another five. Since then, they have recorded a steady four to six sales each week from the site. What's most interesting is that they were approached online by a blind-design firm in Singapore, who were keen to get their designs into the UK and European market, but who were also keen to buy contemporary UK and European designs. As a result, far from considering redundancies, the company is now having to increase its workforce.

Question and answer

How do I know that I can market my company successfully over the internet?

You don't. Until you try, you won't know. But perhaps your real question is, will my particular product or service sell well online? The answer is yes. Some products and services lend themselves naturally to marketing online. Proven examples include books, flowers, music CDs and software. But even services like performance engineering, and products such as fast cars, are all being sold and marketed successfully online.

We could fill this book with real-life companies such as those above. The fact is you don't need a massive marketing budget and a flashy web site to succeed. What you do need in bucket-loads is knowledge and the ability to keep up with, and preferably get ahead of, fast-moving internet trends.

None of those things is difficult to do. We can almost hear you saying, 'Yes, but that's those companies. What about mine?'

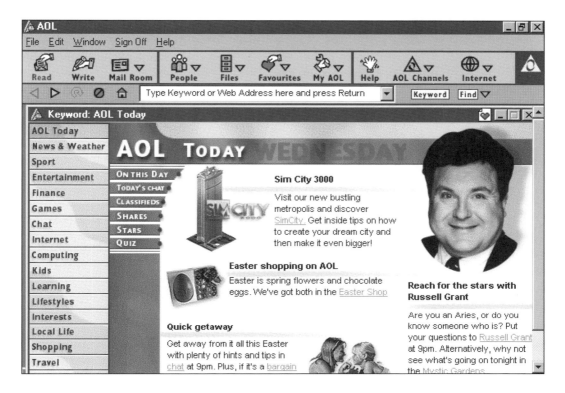

Why your business can be an internet success

If you are already operating a successful business you will be open to the new ways of thinking that the internet requires. You've taken the first step by using this book and perhaps reading about the subject elsewhere. The fact that you stay in business means that you are obviously doing something right. You no doubt have a base of happy customers who buy from you. You actively market to find new customers. You are always on the lookout for new markets to tap into, or extra products and services you can offer. If you can do that offline, you can do the same online. It just requires a new way of thinking, and the courage to grasp the internet and make it work for your company. And it's a two-way street. Many companies are finding that techniques they use to market their businesses offline can also be adapted and used online and vice versa.

Your company can be another internet success story, if you are willing to learn how it works, open your mind to the possibilities, and keep your eye on the ball. If people are buying what you sell in the real world, then there are plenty of them around the world who'll buy it online from you as well.

You've already taken the first step by buying this book. You may also have read some of the business orientated internet magazines. Internet marketing is no more complicated a subject than any other form of marketing. The reason so many companies are complaining that their online marketing isn't working is that they have plunged into online projects before they have really learned the fundamentals of this new global business environment. They take existing ideas and try and force them to work in the online model, and then grumble loudly when they don't. Be different. Take the time to

Fig. 2. America Online. This is its home page for subscribers, redesigned in the early part of 1999 with a more functional and businesslike appearance. AOL has more than 20 million subscribers worldwide.

What will it cost? ....

learn how to do it properly. If you do, your company can be an internet marketing success story.

Why not write in to us (address on back cover) with your experiences? We would look forward to writing about your company in the success stories for the next edition of this book. You have to dive in now. If you don't, then by the time you dip your toe in the water, your rivals may well have built a marina, and established a formidable market lead. So how much will it cost you to market online?

The costs of creating a web site to market your company

By the time you read this it will probably cost more, or perhaps less, than we say. But let's get to grips with some ball-park figures. Here is a rough breakdown of the typical costs of getting started:

1. Internet account and web space, say £500.

2. Web site design, say £850.

3. Ten pages of web site content, say £500.

4. Marketing costs: none except your time. Expect to spend at least several hours a week.

5. Marketing agency. Anything from £100 a month to several thousand pounds a month.

First of all you'll need an internet account so that you can access the internet and obtain some web space. The cost of this varies enormously, as does the quality of the service. A rough average for an account and 10 megabytes of web space – which should be sufficient for most companies – an email account, and registering a domain name for one year will be about £500.

There are now many free internet services, offering web space, and access, some with free phone numbers. These services can be an excellent way of 'putting your toe in the water' to see how you get on. Some offer free web design as well, but what you may find you end up with is an 'identikit' site, which looks like all the others that company has done.

Your next big expense is going to be web-site design and content. The cost of these items will vary according to the needs, size and complexity of your site. A rough average for a site of 10 pages, with some graphics on it, but without all the bells and whistles (that you don't really need anyway), would be about £850. For the content of your 10-page site, you can expect to pay around £500. So your total to get started could typically be about £1,850.

Question and answer

I have a very limited budget and can't afford the amount you quote for getting online. How can I get these things done more cheaply?

You can either do them yourself in the case of the web design and content, or go to a new writer or web designer who will be keen for work and won't charge as much. With service providers, it pays to shop around. You might find it better to start with a small local provider and move up when you can afford it. Or try one of the free services. The cost quoted above of course doesn't include the cost of marketing. Here you have two choices: you can either do it yourself, using books like this one, or you can pay a company to market your site. The do-it-yourself approach is in many ways better. You know your company far better than anyone else does, and you know your market better than anyone else does. But if time is not on your side, then an agency would be a good idea. Just because you don't use one, doesn't mean your competitors (who do) will have a better-marketed company than you. It's what you do, not how much you spend, that counts.

To market your site effectively is going to take several hours a week. You would be wise to budget at least an hour every day. If you feel the cost to your company is going to be too high, then by all means go to an agency. The cost of getting your company online probably isn't as great as you expected, but of course it can be a lot more, depending on how your plans evolve for doing business on the internet. It's best to begin by setting up a small site that you can manage yourself, rather than a large site that you spend more time looking after than you do looking after your customers!

Here are the pros and cons of doing web design and content yourself, or having a company do these things for you. Marketing is something that you may well be able to do better yourself rather than employing an expensive agency. If time is of the essence, however, an agency could be invaluable.

Reasons for doing it yourself

▷ You have complete control over what happens.
▷ You understand your business better than anyone else.
▷ You can find out quickly which marketing tactics work for your company.
▷ You can adapt and change your site as needs be, and as quickly as a situation demands.
▷ It will be cheaper.

Reasons for not doing it yourself

▷ You lack the expertise to design the site and write the content.
▷ You may not be able to communicate what you want effectively.
▷ Your site and content may not look professional.
▷ There is a steep learning curve. You'll need to learn new software and programming languages.

Creating the design and content

Pros of getting someone else to do your design and content

▷ A professional look and feel to your site.

▷ They will be able to suggest ways to improve your site for you. Saves time.

▷ They will be able to add special features to your site if necessary.

▷ Site will be 'road-tested' before it goes online.

Cons of getting someone else to do your design and content

▷ Your designer may be more interested in winning awards than creating an effective site.

▷ Your writer may charge for changes you want done.

▷ Expense. It can be difficult to get an accurate estimate of the eventual total cost.

▷ Difficulties in finding good writers and designers.

▷ You lose some control over the creation of your site.

Case studies

John saves money

John runs a small office supply company. He reckons that if he gets online he can target customers over a wider area, and increase his sales and profits. He sits down and plans exactly what he wants to do with his site, checks out his competitors' sites, and briefs his staff about what he plans to do. He finds an excellent service provider and manages to barter several printer toners, for £150 off his first year using their service. He asks at the local university if any of the students would be willing to design his site for him for a reasonable fee, and several jump at the chance. He also finds an experienced online content writer to create the content for his site. Two months later John's site launches with great success. His first week shows extra sales of £500.

Al overdoes things

Al also runs an office supply company. He's seen some of the office supply sites in the USA, which are large and well produced, and decides he wants one like it. He hires a large web design agency, buys the most expensive web space he can (he believes that it'll make his site run faster than his rivals' sites) and pays an expensive New York-based content writer. He launches his site, but only a few people passing by visit it. Over the next few weeks, a few people drop by, but none buys anything. Al writes the whole thing off, and tells people at his business club that the internet is over-rated at best.

2 What you need for net marketing success

In this chapter we will explore:

▶ *choosing the right service provider for your business*
▶ *web-site design: do it yourself or web design agency?*
▶ *do you need the help of a marketing professional?*
▶ *checklists for service providers, design agencies, and marketing consultancies and companies.*

. . . .

Choosing the right service provider for your business

A quick look through the pages of any of the glossy internet business magazines will leave you bewildered by the choice of internet service providers available. Maybe you already have one, but is it the right one for marketing your business online? As a business user you will have different considerations in mind from those of a private customer. You need an account which:

▷ is very reliable (minimum downtime for repairs or maintenance)

▷ has good access via the phone network (no busy signals, quick transmissions)

▷ has the option of ISDN access if necessary (for much faster transmissions)

▷ has sufficient capacity to hold your site

▷ has an excellent usenet 'feed' (covers as many as possible of the 50,000-plus newsgroups)

▷ has fast access lines both for getting onto the internet and for using it

▷ can guarantee the 'uptime' of your site

▷ has excellent technical support

▷ has necessary 'add-ons' you might need, like secure server facilities (for encrypting commercial transactions or other sensitive information)

▷ perhaps most important of all, understands the needs of your business.

Many businesses are tempted by the so-called 'freespace' and cheap dial-in accounts that are widely advertised. For business purposes these are all but useless. They make your company look amateurish and give the immediate impression that you don't much value your online clients and customers.

Registering your domain name..

Ideally you need to have your own domain name. A domain name is the part of your email address which comes after the @ symbol. For instance, the email address of the author of this book is:

sara@imarketingservices.co.uk

The domain name is

imarketingservices.co.uk

You can choose a variety of endings to your domain name, for example:

.co.uk

which shows you're a UK-based company, or:

.com

Fig. 3. UK DomainNames is a web site where you can register your new business domain name (provided the name has not already been taken by someone else). It's easy to register offshore domain names, too.

which is mostly used in the USA. This is often the preferred option for UK companies, since it implies an international company. You may prefer to use '.co.uk' if you wish to get across that your business is UK-based.

You can buy your domain name from your service provider, since many of them include the cost of registering a domain name in their packages. Or you can go to any one of many domain name services (DNS). The choice

is yours. Do shop around, though, as charges vary a good deal. Most important of all, register your domain name now! The longer you leave it, the less chance you will have of getting the name you want, as many people are now finding when trying to register. There is a global rush going on to capture good domain names. Many companies register every conceivable way of spelling their company name, to stop anyone else using something similar.

If you already have a domain name, most service providers will transfer it to your new account with them. So how do you choose a service provider? There is no single answer to this. It depends on your needs. Most companies will need the following:

▷ at least 10 megabytes of web space

▷ a dial-up account with at least 5 mail boxes, preferably more. 'Unlimited email addresses' gives you the maximum flexibility because then you can have all kinds of handy email addresses such as:

  sales@mysite.co.uk
  feedback@mysite.co.uk
  jsmith@mysite.co.uk
  catalogues@mysite.co.uk
  orders@mysite.co.uk
  enquiries@mysite.co.uk

▷ guaranteed 'uptime' for your web site (should be for at least 95 per cent of the time.

▷ a reliable news feed

▷ a reliable email feed

▷ a fast server (a server is the computer that holds or 'hosts' your web site, allowing others to access it)

▷ domain name registration or transfer

▷ support for certain software if you intend building your web site yourself. For example, if you intend to use Microsoft FrontPage authoring software, your access provider needs to support its server extensions.

Most service providers provide everything you need in a single package which you buy from them each year. Many expect you to pay for this upfront, but if you can it is better to pay it quarterly. Then, if you have any problems, you can quit the service without undue cost.

Which service provider should I choose?

This is a complicated question, not helped by the constant take-overs and mergers in the industry. As a general rule, the larger the company the better. They are less likely to be taken over (with disruptive changes to the service) and often offer extras that smaller companies cannot offer. Their infrastructure is often more advanced and they have access to the fastest lines.

Fig. 4. Virgin Net's home page for its subscribers. Virgin are developing a new range of online services for business. Its basic service is now free.

The drawback with using a larger company is the lack of personal service, and often the higher cost. Smaller local service providers can be a good starting point, but many are more geared towards consumer access and may not understand the needs of your business. The plus side to using them is that they are often cheaper and offer a much higher level of personal service. Service providing is a very competitive industry, so a bit of haggling can often work wonders. Many companies have special offers on at one time or another, but make sure they are offering something you need.

Also make sure that any guarantees they give are in writing. This is vitally important. A member of their staff may say one thing over the phone and then send you something different. This is especially important when it comes to price. If they offer you a special deal, ask them to confirm the details in writing before you send them your purchase order.

Checklist

1. Make sure your service provider will provide you with, at the very least, the basics of a commercial account, as listed above.

2. Get all the terms of service from them in writing.

3. Play one service provider off against another to try and get a discount.

4. If they refuse to guarantee 'uptime' for your web site, typically 95 per cent of the time, then go somewhere else.

5. Only buy what you need. Buying ahead of yourself can prove a false economy.

6. If you want a cheaper service, with more personal advice and care, choose a local or small service provider.

7. If you can afford to, use a larger service provider for the advantages of consistency, quality, reliability and durability of service.

8. Check what technical support you are entitled to.

9. Make sure that your software is compatible with their system; for example, if you are an Apple Mac user.

10. Check their domain name registration costs against the competition.

Questions and answers

Is it vital that I have my own domain name?

It isn't vital, but it does look more professional to visit a site at:

> www.imarketingservices.co.uk

than to visit one at:

> www.aras.demon.co.uk/imarketingservices

Which is better, a large service provider or a smaller one?

Smaller ones generally have fewer facilities, such as fast access lines to other parts of the world. But they offer a much higher standard of customer care, and often have excellent technical support lines. Larger

Fig. 5. CompuServe is another of the top internet service and content providers. Like AOL, it was one of the first such providers, and has developed much web-based content of its own.

service providers have the facilities, but can sometimes be impersonal and are often more expensive.

Web-site design: do it yourself or use an agency?

This question has had more articles and features written about it than just about any other subject on the internet. Yes, it is an important question, as the first thing your visitor sees is your web-site design. Which method you decide on will depend on several factors. These include:

▶ whether you have people with graphic design skills in your company

▶ your budget

▶ what you intend to do on your site.

A vigorous debate has been raging about the first of these. If you have a graphic designer on your company staff, they will no doubt be excellent at designing for print. Designing for the web is a different matter. It uses the same skills, but in a different way. Some designers suit the internet medium better than others, and the only way to find out is to get them busy. In our experience we've found that graphic designers can design excellent pages, once they are aware of how the internet works and its interactive potential (for example, hyperlinks, email facilities, online forms, hit counters, and secure transmissions).

Fig. 6. Demon Internet. Demon offers to get your business online with commercial web space at an affordable price. Demon led the way among UK independents, but at the end of 1998 became a subsidiary of Scottish Telecom.

Your budget is also an important consideration. If money is tight, then you can either do the work yourself, or find a young agency or hungry freelance to do your site for you. A web design agency that understands

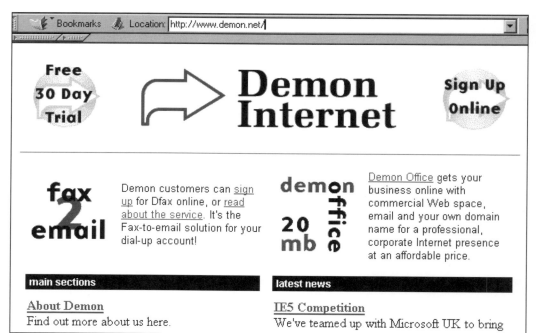

your business and has a reputation for building excellent business sites is a wise investment, provided you can afford the fees.

The pros of using an agency

An agency will have:

▶ extensive experience in coding and designing sites

▶ excellent knowledge of the online business environment

▶ the ability to create the specific interactive elements you need

▶ access to experts in their field

▶ the possibility they can maintain the site for you.

The cons of using an agency

▶ the expense

▶ some agencies are more interested in the 'art' of web sites than the commercial realities

▶ they may want to impose their ideas and ideals on to your site

▶ they don't understand your business as well as you do.

This brings us to DIY. Many books and magazines scorn the idea that a company can design and build its own site effectively. We don't agree with this view. Yes, many terrible sites have been built by companies doing it themselves, but equally many terrible ones have been paid for by some unfortunate company using a web design agency.

The pros of DIY web-site design

▶ You have complete control over the process.

▶ You understand your business and its market better than anyone.

▶ You understand your customers' needs better than anyone.

▶ It saves money.

The cons of DIY web-site design

▶ You can end up with a very tacky site, through lack of experience.

▶ It can cost you money in terms of lost sales.

▶ There is a steep learning curve.

▶ Staff will be tied up designing the site instead of doing their other work.

If you decide to follow the DIY route, you will have to learn to use a web-design package, or learn HTML (the coding language of the web). It will take longer, and the end result may not look professional. This said, you can learn a huge amount designing and building your own site, and you have total control over what happens. Your staff will learn valuable skills for the future, and you will have a better understanding of how web technology ticks, which can be exploited in the future.

Fig. 7. Owned by
Macromedia,
Dreamweaver has
established itself as one of
the most popular web-
authoring packages,
at a price of around £200.

If you decide to take this route, then you'll need the following as a minimum:

▷ several good books on HTML, or you could attend a course

▷ a web page design package, such as Dreamweaver, GoLive, Corel Webmaster, or Microsoft FrontPage

▷ plenty of time

▷ a clear understanding of basic design principles

▷ a clear idea of what you want your site to look like.

Fig. 8. GoLive is another
popular and well-regarded
web-authoring package,
available at a budget price.
It is owned by Adobe,
famous for Adobe Acrobat
software.

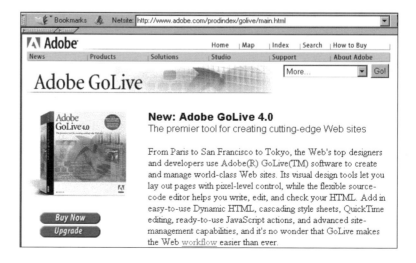

Choosing an agency to do the work for you, though, can be just as pro-
blematic! Anyone can learn to code HTML and call themselves a web
designer, and many do. You have two choices, you can either go to a freelance web-site designer, or you can go to an agency which employs
several people. The freelance will be cheaper, and probably more accom-
modating to any changes you need doing. Many of the best designers
work freelance, so ask around to find out who's good. An agency will
have staff who have trained in graphic design and web-site coding.
They often have the latest technologies you can put on your site, and
considerable experience. The problem is they are often expensive, and
can be more than a little self-interested, though this is changing.

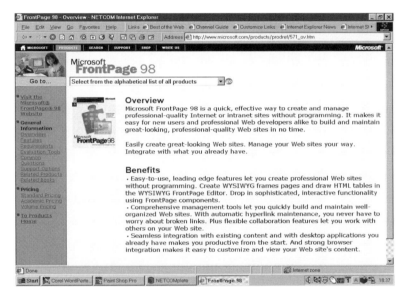

Fig. 9. Microsoft naturally
has its own web-
authoring package, called
FrontPage. Priced at under
£100, it can handle
frames, and has probably
sold more copies than any
similar software. There is
also a cut-down version
called FrontPage Express.

Checklist for choosing a web-site designer (freelance)

1. Find out how long they have been designing for the web.

2. Ask to see some sites they have worked on.

3. Contact the company whose site they designed and ask them a few
   questions.

4. Make sure they give you a flat fee, with no hidden charges.

5. Ask to see written (not email) testimonials from their happy clients.

Checklist for choosing a web design agency

▷ Ask to see their client list. Do you know any of the companies on the
   list?

▷ Do they understand your industry sector, or are they generalists?
   Which client on their list seems closest to what you are aiming to do?

Fig. 10. NETStart is a package provided by one of the UK's leading ISPs, Netcom.

▷ Does the agency specialise in any particular type of site? What evidence can they show of this?

▷ Bigger isn't always better, so ask around for recommendations of good agencies. Be as thorough as you can. Once you have become involved with an agency, you may find it difficult from a technical point of view to disentangle yourself and your web site.

▷ Find out how long their staff have trained in web-site design and whether they have any formal graphic design qualifications (for example, college certificates or diplomas).

▷ Ask about fees and any extra charges. Do they have a standard printed tariff of charges? What is their hourly rate for general work on the web site? Are there any recurring monthly, quarterly or annual fees?

Further tips

(a) Do shop around for agencies. Some include items such as revisions in the price, whereas others charge extra.

(b) Ask them about web-site content.

(c) If they offer a copywriting service, do they use professional writers, or are the designers themselves writing the material?

(d) Make sure you have a clear idea in your mind what you want your site to do and how it should look.

(e) Be open to their suggestions, but don't allow them to push you into doing things that you don't want or like. Be assertive if necessary.

(f) Read the superb book, *Web Pages That Suck: Learning Good Design by Looking at Bad Design*, by Vincent Flanders and Michael Willis, before you either DIY your site, or have an agency do it for you. This way you will become aware of the pitfalls and problems.

Can the marketing professionals help you?

Question and answer

I would like to do our own web site. Which software package would be best for me?

The best is probably Microsoft FrontPage. This has been described as the package for the 'businessperson in a rush' and is an easy-to-use piece of software. It supports the major add-ons for web sites. It is probably the most widely used such package in the world. It costs under £100, or you can use a free cut-down version called Microsoft FrontPage Express. There are various other packages, some simpler than this or more complicated. Keep an eye on the reviews pages of the internet business magazines, and ask other people which package they like using, and why. What are its strengths? What are its limitations?

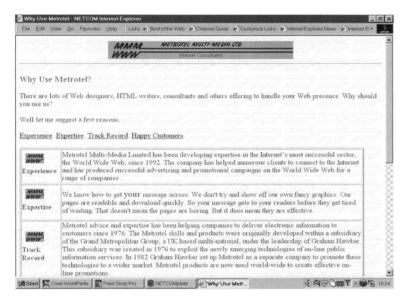

Fig. 11. Metrotel Multi-Media is another UK firm offering expertise in advertising and marketing products and services on the internet.

Do you need the help of a marketing professional?

The internet marketing profession has suffered a lot from people making claims that they can't possibly live up to, which has damaged many professional people's reputations. As the market is developing, internet marketing professionals are divided into roughly two camps:

1. Internet marketing consultants – they will help you decide how to market your company and build your brand online. There are more of these than the other category. If you have the resources in-house to market your company or want to market your company yourself, and want some guidance, these are the people to deal with.

2. Internet marketing companies – these can advise you on the best way to market and build your company's brand online, just as the consultants can. The difference is that these companies can also do the actual marketing and support for you, leaving you to simply process the orders that come in.

Choosing an internet marketing consultancy...........................

So, which one do you need for your company?

You need an internet marketing consultant if:

1. You have adequate resources to market your company yourself online.

2. You want to market your company online yourself.

3. You need an internet marketing strategy.

4. You feel you need the expertise of an online marketing expert.

You need an internet marketing company if:

1. You lack the resources inside your company to market it effectively yourself.

2. You lack online marketing expertise in your company.

3. You don't have the time to market your company online, but feel it is an important part of your marketing strategy as a whole.

As with web design, this is an industry without recognised authorities to help you make the right decision. When you have decided which you need to use in your company, then comes the tough part, finding the right company.

Since the market is so new, very few companies specialise in one particular industry, but many deal with several companies from a specific sector, so they could be your first port of call. If you're looking for a consultant, size isn't always everything. Some large management and marketing consultancies have tagged on internet marketing as a saleable extra to their portfolios, believing that there isn't much difference between what they're doing and internet marketing. This is untrue, so be sure to check that the company you choose is preferably a dedicated internet marketing company. Independent internet marketing consultancies can often be the best bet for companies to go to (unless you happen to be the size of Heinz).

Choosing an internet marketing consultancy

Here are a few pointers to choosing an internet marketing consultancy:

1. Are they a dedicated internet marketing consultancy?

2. How long have their people worked at internet marketing?

3. What is the average result that the company produces?

4. Do they offer any guarantees?

5. Who are their clients? Get in touch with them and ask them some key questions.

Internet marketing companies are relatively new in the internet marketing field. At the present time many companies prefer to do their own marketing, only to find it far more time-consuming than they first imagined, and so they hand it over to an internet marketing company to do it for them.

Though a lot of these companies only serve very large customers, there is a growing band of companies who deal with medium and large-sized organisations. These companies will do all your marketing for you, from maintaining your web site, to watching over it, posting into newsgroups and mailing lists, answering customer queries, promoting your site on other sites and in newsletters and magazines. Their services are not the cheapest option. You are paying not only for the time they take to carry out these tasks, but also for their expertise in doing the marketing.

Choosing an internet marketing company

Here are a few pointers to choosing an internet marketing company:

▷ How experienced are their people at marketing companies online?

▷ Do they produce consistent results? If so, what are they?

▷ Ask others who have used these companies which ones they found the best.

▷ Keep an eye on internet business magazines for overviews of which companies do what.

▷ Read newsgroups or subscribe to mailing lists to find out about internet marketing companies and their abilities.

Fig. 12. Web Pages That Suck. A great site to visit for anyone building a web site.

Case studies . . . .

Question and answer

Can I do my own internet marketing and still be as effective as a professional service?

Yes, but it will eat into your time. An internet marketing company, for example, may spend as much as six hours a day doing nothing but marketing your company online, checking newsgroups, sites and so on. Few companies can afford to have their employees tied up for this length of time each day. With all your professionals in place (or not, as the case may be) you're ready for the next step!

Case studies

Bob's big blunder

Bob is in charge of his company's new internet marketing strategy, and he's keen to show he's up to the job. He doesn't know much about the internet, or design or writing for that matter. He rings up several web design agencies and internet marketing agencies to try to pick their brains free of charge for advice. Most of them are not impressed. Bob builds the site and starts marketing it online. But he finds little success. At the end of the first month, only ten people have visited the site. In the end he contacts some more companies and has the site professionally redesigned and rewritten.

Carol's cautious success

Carol looks after her company's marketing communications and has been asked to prepare the company's web site, and devise a marketing plan for it. She buys some magazines and a few books and spends the weekend reading up. Next, she contacts several web design agencies and visits several of them. But she isn't particularly impressed with any she sees. So she consults an internet mailing list for advice on which one to choose. Someone recommends a small agency who have worked in her company's field; after a couple of meetings she gives them the job. Her boss is very impressed with her hard work and with how she has negotiated an excellent deal. (For more on using online mailing lists, see Chapter 10.)

Fig. 13. Macromedia has established itself as a leading brand of internet software, such as Shockwave and Flash, which allow animated effects to be added to web sites.

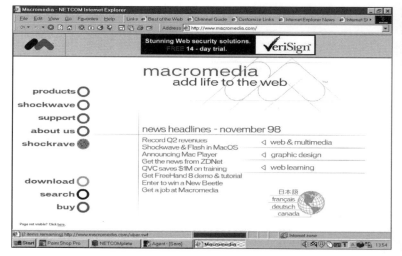

3 Don't forget your map! Planning for online success

In this chapter we will explore:

▶ *what you want to achieve from your online marketing*
▶ *checking out your online competition*
▶ *discovering the right online niche − a step-by-step guide*
▶ *devising a strategy for success − a checklist of the key items.*

. . . .

What do you want to achieve from your online marketing?

Marketing plans are essential in the 'real' world of business and are just as important in the online world, if not more so. Your marketing plan will become a 'living' document − as everything on the internet moves so quickly, it's easy to get left behind.

Your marketing plan needs to cover several areas:

▷ the content of your web site: what will be updated each month, and what will only be updated occasionally

▷ your main areas for marketing − the web, newsgroups and so on

▷ your competitors' sites

▷ regular marketing tactics you'll use, such as press releases and newsletters

▷ generating offline interest in your site

▷ and most important of all, what you want to achieve with your marketing.

Many companies would answer that they want to make millions in profits from their web site, and while that's an admirable goal, it isn't altogether very realistic to start off with. Are you going to use your web site to build your brand image? To generate online sales? To generate sales enquiries?

You can do all of these things, though that will require a detailed plan, which is beyond the scope of this book. To help you decide what you want to achieve from your online marketing, let's take a quick look at what each of them would entail, in terms of marketing.

Brand image on the internet ....

Online brand-building

If you want to build your brand image online, you'll need to spend a great deal of time online. The most successful brand-building is done by companies who give a 'community' feel to their site. One of the best examples of this is Geocities, which is almost an online country. All its members are bound by the community feel that Geocities gives them. They can chat, message each other, buy books from Amazon.com, all from within Geocities online.

Geocities has built its now well-known brand around its community. Mention the name to anyone who has used the internet for some time, and they'll know exactly who you're talking about.

Amazon.com is another example of excellent branding; even many non-internet users know that it's a large online bookstore.

Fig. 14. Amazon is an outstanding example of successful business branding and niche-building on the internet. The company is barely four years old, and its sales already exceed $300m a year. What other bookselling company on the planet could point to such astounding growth?

In both cases most of the hard work in branding these companies came from the users themselves, and from the companies' excellent online service. To brand your site, you'll have to do the same. Offer real involvement to your visitors, develop your site into the ideal place for your customers to come and visit, chat in and so on. To do this, you'll need to create a well-designed site which has high quality content and is regularly updated. It will also need forums, mailing lists, special areas for members and other items.

Then you need to make sure that your web site's name appears wherever your customers are on the web. This may involve buying banner ads on various areas of the web, encouraging your visitors to mention your site to others, posting relevant, helpful messages into newsgroups and mailing lists, and sending articles to e-zines (electronic magazines) and

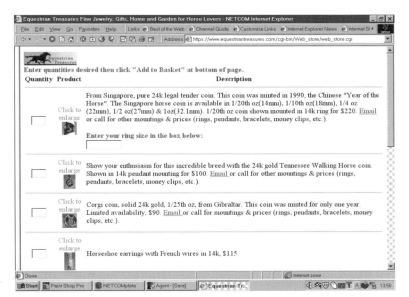

Fig. 15. Equestrian Treasures. Another example of internet site niching, this site sells unusual horse-related items.

newsletters. This is just the start! Brand-building is a major undertaking, but it can also be very profitable if you get it right.

Spend some time on the most popular community brand-building sites, and keep an eye on the web and internet in general for mentions of them and ads by them.

Fig. 16. Microsoft's Support pages. If you are offering online support, this is the site to emulate.

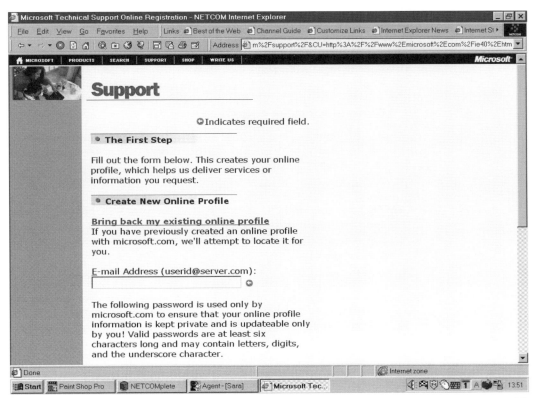

Generating online sales

If you want to generate online sales (I'll take it that you've got the secure server and credit card facilities in place), take a look at Amazon.com, a superb example of online sales. Their ordering system is simplicity itself to use, and they keep in touch with their customers — they tell you when your order has been accepted, when they've shipped it, and even give you package-tracking information if relevant.

The key to success, here, is to give the right amount of sales and factual information to the visitor. If you're intending selling to countries outside your own, you should price your goods in various currencies, and give shipping rates for all of them.

A site aimed at selling something also needs to have a community feel, but in a different way. Your site should be a shopping experience for your customers, something unique, interesting, fun even. This will take expertise on the design and content side, so if this is what you want to do, then get a professional web-site designer and an online content copywriter to do the work for you.

The best form of marketing for this kind of site is word of mouth, so your service must be excellent. There are various sites that are dedicated to helping people find a widget or whatever, so getting *your* site on the relevant ones is vital. E-zines, mailing lists and newsletters are all marketing tools you'll need to keep customers coming back. Customer loyalty schemes, special offers, discounts and so on are also useful, and can be used in your marketing.

Newsgroups, mailing lists and e-zines which cover your subject are also areas where you can bring the customers to your site.

Generating sales enquiries

If sales enquiries are what you're looking for, then you still need to build that community feel. There's no getting away from it. Many companies use hard sell to try and get the enquiries flowing, but what works in the 'real' world doesn't really work online.

You need a more subtle approach, tempting your visitor in with information that they will value. Forums and the like are popular on this type of site, and are excellent ways of doing some market research; you'll be amazed what potential customers tell you in forums.

A site like this also needs something a bit special to draw people in. Mortgage calculators, mini-spreadsheets to work out the cost of mailings and so on have all been used successfully. Try to think of something your customers would find useful, and then use it as a marketing point for the site.

As regards details of your products and services, the internet business community is divided into two camps. One camp says that you should

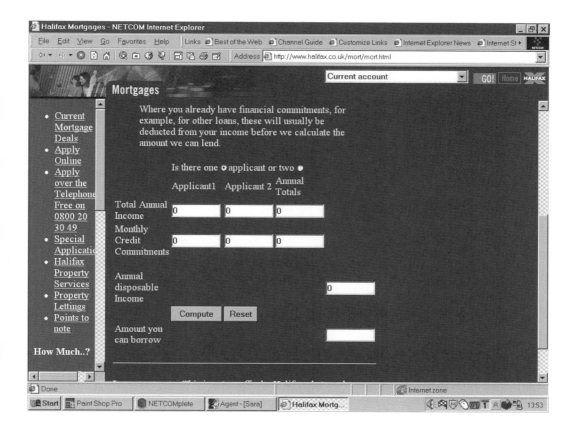

Fig. 17. The Halifax is one of the UK's biggest mortgage lenders. Its web site will calculate a mortgage offer for potential borrowers, based on their income and other details they key in.

give as much information as possible about your product or service, the other camp says that you should be more coy, giving out some of the benefits and results you can deliver, rather than going the whole way.

The choice is yours, and it is probably better to look at your offline marketing to see which has worked best for you in the past and take it from there. For this kind of marketing, you need to almost blanket market your target market, in much the same way as a company that wants to build its brand online.

Questions and answers

You say that a marketing plan is a 'living document'. Does that mean there's no point actually writing it down in the conventional sense?

Not at all. It's just as important to write it all down. By a 'living document' I mean that it has the flexibility to change with the changes that the internet may bring to your company. You might find a new set of sites, or technology might appear that can help your marketing even more. If your marketing plan is too rigid it won't be able to take that into account.

Isn't it possible to brand, bring in sales enquiries and bring in sales all at the same, using the same marketing?

In some ways, yes. But you may end up with a lower quality of customer than you would like, not to mention the fact that your poor customer could end up confused about exactly what you do want out of him or her.

Working out your competitors' online marketing strategies

No matter how well you niche your business online, there's still going to be competition. If your competitors are already online then it is vital that you discover where and how they are marketing their site, so you can make the necessary adjustments to your marketing.

This isn't as difficult as it sounds, but it does take time to do. So if you're short of time or can't spare the staff to do this, there are various agencies on the net who'll do it for you. They operate in a similar way to a newspaper clippings service. Here are several ways you can keep an eye on your competitors' marketing strategies:

Fig. 18. Using a search engine (in this case Yahoo!) to identify competitors or suppliers in a particular industry. Click on any of the underlined words to find out more detailed information.

▷ Use Deja (www.deja.com) to do a detailed search of usenet for words, company names, product names and so on associated with your competitors.

▷ Use the main search engines to do a similar search. However, don't just use one engine, use several of them. They all list companies in different ways.

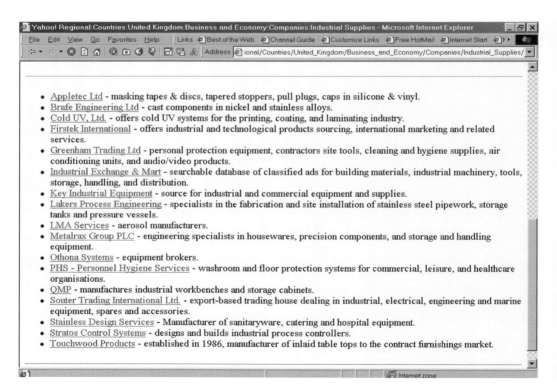

- Appletec Ltd - masking tapes & discs, tapered stoppers, pull plugs, caps in silicone & vinyl.
- Brafe Engineering Ltd - cast components in nickel and stainless alloys.
- Cold UV, Ltd. - offers cold UV systems for the printing, coating, and laminating industry.
- Firstek International - offers industrial and technological products sourcing, international marketing and related services.
- Greenham Trading Ltd - personal protection equipment, contractors site tools, cleaning and hygiene supplies, air conditioning units, and audio/video products.
- Industrial Exchange & Mart - searchable database of classified ads for building materials, industrial machinery, tools, storage, handling, and distribution.
- Key Industrial Equipment - source for industrial and commercial equipment and supplies.
- Lakers Process Engineering - specialists in the fabrication and site installation of stainless steel pipework, storage tanks and pressure vessels.
- LMA Services - aerosol manufacturers.
- Metalrax Group PLC - engineering specialists in housewares, precision components, and storage and handling equipment.
- Othona Systems - equipment brokers.
- PHS - Personnel Hygiene Services - washroom and floor protection systems for commercial, leisure, and healthcare organisations.
- QMP - manufactures industrial workbenches and storage cabinets.
- Souter Trading International Ltd. - export-based trading house dealing in industrial, electrical, engineering and marine equipment, spares and accessories.
- Stainless Design Services - Manufacturer of sanitaryware, catering and hospital equipment.
- Stratos Control Systems - designs and builds industrial process controllers.
- Touchwood Products - established in 1986, manufacturer of inlaid table tops to the contract furnishings market.

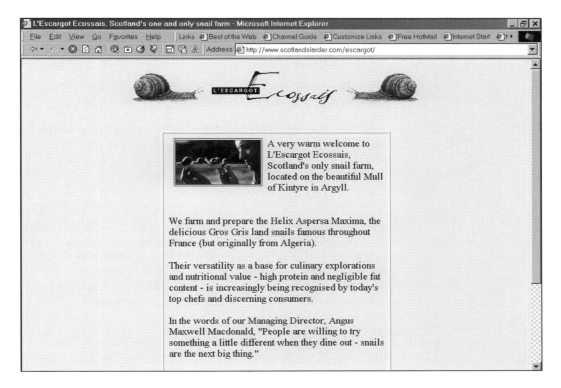

A very warm welcome to L'Escargot Ecossais, Scotland's only snail farm, located on the beautiful Mull of Kintyre in Argyll.

We farm and prepare the Helix Aspersa Maxima, the delicious Gros Gris land snails famous throughout France (but originally from Algeria).

Their versatility as a base for culinary explorations and nutritional value - high protein and negligible fat content - is increasingly being recognised by today's top chefs and discerning consumers.

In the words of our Managing Director, Angus Maxwell Macdonald, "People are willing to try something a little different when they dine out - snails are the next big thing."

▷ Then search on any specialist search engines related to your industry.

Fig. 19. L'Escargot Ecossais – a good example of a successful niche business on the internet.

▷ Check out their web sites. Spend some time going round the site, seeing what it has that yours doesn't. Check out any forums that your competitors' web sites have, to see what people are saying about the site.

▷ Watch out for banner ads which advertise your competitors.

▷ Subscribe to relevant newsgroups and watch out for postings.

▷ Do the same for newsletters, e-zines and mailing lists.

▷ Ask your customers where they've seen your competitors advertising online.

These checks need to be done continually, otherwise your competitors may find a new way of marketing which you haven't tried yet. Each time you carry out this exercise you'll end up with a lot of data about what they are doing. Though you won't know how successful their marketing is, if they keep doing the same things then they're either not really interested in marketing themselves, or their marketing is working so well, they don't need to try anything else.

The best way of keeping your competitors on their toes is to niche your site extremely well; this makes it much more difficult for them to compete with you.

Finding your niche on the net ....

Question and answer

My competitors are much larger than I am and can afford to market their businesses much better than I can. So what use is this to me?

A lot of use. The beauty of the internet is that you can have millions for your marketing budget and still lose out to a smaller rival. What you don't have in money you can make up for in time, which makes this sort of information-gathering so important.

Discovering your online niche – a step-by-step guide

Niches are important offline, but they are even more vital online. A niche that works well for you in the 'real' world may be too wide to work well online. This is a common mistake which many companies make. The internet is a massive marketing arena and, with web sites appearing every day, it forces you to tighten your niche beyond what you would normally do in the 'real' world. So how can you discover your niche online?

Fig. 20. *Niche* is an online magazine devoted entirely to the practicalities of building a business niche on the internet. Take a look, and be prepared to change your way of thinking.

Step 1
Find out why your customers buy from you. Ask them to be very specific about why they do. Rather than getting an answer like 'your company is very professional', ask them exactly how they define professionalism. If you already have a site online, ask your visitors who buy or enquire exactly why they did so. What made them want to?

Step 2
Look for any patterns in this information. For example, let's say you run a photo shop, which sells cameras and does film processing. You may find that your market can be divided into several segments, such as semi-professionals, professionals, hobbyist, and the 'must-have' hobbyist.

Within these segments you might find that your customers all come to your company because your staff really know what they're talking about and that you offer special processing requirements they need. These patterns in your segments can help you find different niches to exploit. For example, the professionals and semi-professionals appreciate your special processing abilities and fast turnaround, so you could niche yourself to them as a company who specialises in that.

Step 3
You may well have identified several niches, and each of these can be catered for on your site. The only limit to this is how much you're willing to spend on web-site space, and how much time/money you're willing to spend on marketing. The niches you've found might seem too small, but online they aren't as small as they might be offline, simply because of the way people gather into small communities online.

Step 4
Organise your site according to the niches you want to exploit, and then organise your marketing so that it addresses each of the niches you've identified. You may find that some niches need less marketing than others.

Step 5
Exploit the niche for all its worth. In the photography example, you could perhaps have links on your site to the other niches your marketing is aimed at.

Step 6
Build the perception in your customers' minds that you are 'the' company for that niche. Do this by targeting your marketing carefully in the places they are most likely to be.

Extra help

If you're still stuck, take a look online at your target market. Read what they read, visit the sites they go to and read the forums they read. You'll always find a worthwhile niche by doing this.

Summary

To sum up, to find your niche online you need to:

▷ Find out why your customers are buying from you. Identify any hidden needs or wants you can fill.

▷ Look for patterns in the information they give you. These could be exploitable niches.

▷ Organise your web site so it caters for the niches you wish to go after.

▷ Exploit the niche with links to other relevant products or services you sell.

▷ Target your marketing at them in such a way as to build a perception that you are 'the' company for that niche.

Devising an online marketing plan......................................

If you get stuck, get on the net and read what your visitors read. This way you can find out a lot about them and any hidden needs or wants they may have.

Check there's a demand for what you're selling!

Question and answer

We're a medium-sized company, and it simply wouldn't be economic for us to chase small niches. How can we niche ourselves?

As some of the largest companies in the world are discovering, size isn't everything online. People gather into communities, and within those communities are niches waiting to be exploited. You need to think globally, rather than just in your own patch. Small niches might not work in your home area, but they can work very well online.

Devising your strategy for success

Now you understand the basic components of your marketing approach, you can start to put it together into a marketing plan that will work for your company. Here's a checklist of the most important steps:

1. Decide what your marketing goal is. Is it to build a brand image? Get sales enquiries? Get online sales?

2. Don't write your marketing plan in stone. The internet is constantly evolving, and so must your marketing plan.

3. Set aside a specific budget for your internet marketing.

4. Decide what the content on your site will be and how often it will be updated.

5. Decide what the main areas for your marketing will be. This depends on what you hope to achieve.

6. Check out your competitors' sites, and try and see how they're marketing their company and site.

Cultivate your online niche or niches. Market those niches as much as you can. But do make sure they are likely to be profitable before you start. Keep your eye on the road.

The information superhighway is full of new technologies, which will either help or hinder your marketing. It's important to stay with these technologies and preferably ahead of them. This is probably the most time-consuming part of your marketing. Your marketing plan will evolve as your online role changes. Don't make the mistake many hundreds of companies have made before you, and fail to plan. Otherwise you're planning to fail.

Case studies

Go It Alone Gary

Gary is very excited about the possibilities for marketing his company online. He dives straight in, posting into newsgroups, mailing lists, and anywhere else. He gets lots of new visitors to his site, but not many sales. He puts this down to not marketing enough and does even more.

After a year Gary gives up when a competitor finds a deep and profitable niche, which Gary realises he should have spotted. If only he'd made a marketing plan!

Malcolm . . the Marketing Marvel

Malcolm is also very excited about the online possibilities for his business. But he's been burnt before in the 'real' world so he spends several weeks working out what will work and what won't. He's not entirely sure whether he's totally on the right track, but figures he can change his plans if necessary.

He discovers three profitable niches that the 'big boys' have ignored and proceeds to build his brand and business image to those niches. He soon has to move his web site to a faster server to cope with the demand for his site, and his sales go up nicely, too.

4 I never knew that!
How to create customer-friendly
content for your web site

In this chapter we will explore:

▶ *how to decide what you want to put on your site*
▶ *12 essential items to have on your web site*
▶ *how to overcome your customers' information fatigue*
▶ *publicity-friendly content tactics*
▶ *the secrets of securing qualified leads and sales from your web site.*

How to decide what to put on your site

Knowing what you want to do online is one third of the job done. Now comes the fun part, deciding what to put on your web site. It's tempting to put photos of yourself and your staff on your site, some information about how great your company is, how your customers love you and so on. After all, everyone does it – take a look at a few company sites: plenty of photographs, but not much in the way of sales. Why?

Because it's terminally boring for the visitor. To be blunt, visitors don't care what you look like and they couldn't care less that your company has been in business for 20 years. Here's one of the best kept net secrets:

▷ Potential customers go online to find solutions to their problems.

That piece of information alone could be worth thousands of pounds in profits to your company. And it's also the reason why so many web sites fail to make their owners any money. The internet is one huge problem-solving arena, except few people have realised that. The ones who have keep quiet about it and enjoy the financial benefits. So, put aside your pride in your company and its achievements, and think solutions to your customers' problems. Your bank balance will love you for it.

The content of your web site is what matters. People will forgive lacklustre design if the content of the site delivers the goods or services that solve their problems. And if you get your content spot on, they'll buy from you. Here's how you can deliver the goods and make the sales:

1. Make your site 'the' resource on your industry or niche.

2. Be unique, exploit your online niche to the full.

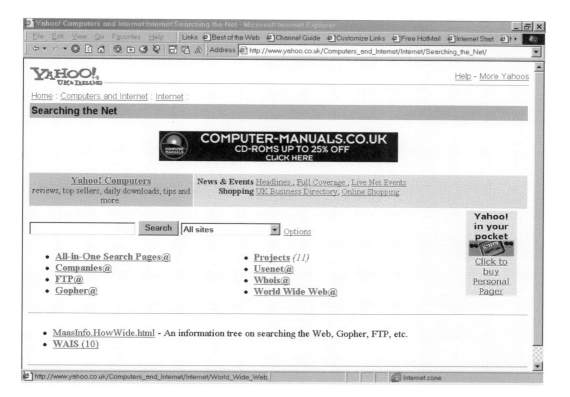

Fig. 21. Computer-Manuals use banner ads to help attract people to their site. In this case, if you go to a computer page on Yahoo!, you see their ad.

Tread the fine line between giving too much information away (after all, you want them to buy the solution from you, not get it for free) and giving too little information away. Easy? No, but together we'll get it right. Once again, here are the most important questions you must ask yourself about the content of your web site.

Checklist

▷ Think solutions to problems. What can you put on your web site that will help your potential customers?

▷ Become a resource. What information can you put on your web site that will make it the obvious place to visit when a potential customer has a problem?

▷ What can you offer potential customers that your competitors can't? One clue here: competing on price on the net isn't a good idea. Why? Because exchange rate differences let competitors in other countries undercut you.

▷ What unique features will you have on your web site? More detail about this one coming up.

▷ Why-Why? Why should a visitor visit your site instead of another one? Why should potential customers buy from you? Ask yourself the Why-Why question again and again about your web site content. Put yourself into your customers' minds and ask - Why? - about your content ideas.

43

What you should have on your site ....

Question and answer

How can my company find out what sort of content would work on our site?

The easiest way is to simply ask your customers. A quick survey of them will soon give you plenty of ideas. Also check out newsgroups and forums your customers read. They can also give you valuable ideas.

Twelve essential items to have on your web site

So what could you put on your site that would not only solve your customers' problems but also increase your sales? Here are twelve essential content items you could put on your web site:

Fig. 22. The Rocking Horse Shop. This site is a fine example of both a great niche and a site with a good balance of sales information and general information – all of which helps sales.

1. **High-quality information**. Or, even better, **hard-to-get information**. On the internet, information rules OK, especially quality information. There's always some new information you can find and use on your site; keep up to date with the latest trends in your business sector and put them on your web site.

2. If you want to go one step further and make some money from your site, offer **personalised information** to your visitors in return for more details about them or a subscription fee (more on this in a later chapter). This is also a great way to pre-qualify your sales leads.

Fig. 23. Linux is 'the' software of the moment. Red Hat's site allows you to order from them easily.

3. **Easy-to-read content**. This one isn't a 'thing', but it's very important. Try to keep your content to a single web page, with a link or button between the pages. One of the most off-putting things on a web site is being faced with a whole page of text. Break it up into 'chunks' of text, with plenty of space around each chunk.

4. **Be interactive**. People on the internet often describe themselves as the 'net community' and one of the reasons the net is so popular is because of its community feel. The companies who've been successful on the net understand that, and cater for it. You can too.

5. Another great interactive tactic is **forums**. These are special areas of your web site where people can drop by, write a message, read some other messages, reply to those, and so on. Each message appears on the screen, so that everyone can read it and, if they like, comment on it. These forums are very popular with visitors, and also allow your staff to reply and, if necessary, to help someone out, which boosts your company's online image and helps sales. If you can, have your forum moderated. Have one of your staff in charge of making sure that the messages in the forum are related to your subject matter. Online forums are a favourite target for the 'get-rich-quick' brigade, who will happily fill your forum with junk messages. A moderator can get rid of those messages before they appear.

6. Have an **'agony aunt'** on your site. Seriously. This is an under-used tactic, but a highly effective one. Instead of answering questions about dubious magazines under the bed, and rampant sex drives, your 'agony aunt' answers questions relating to your field of interest. Questions your visitors send in by email can be answered by one of your team of expert staff. People love reading about other people's problems, even if they aren't sex related.

7. **Things for free**. If there's one thing that companies online grumble about most, it's the internet's so-called 'freebie' culture. But you can use this to your advantage. Offer a free newsletter, report, a piece of software, consultation – anything you can think of. Make it something valuable and helpful, but not so valuable and helpful that they don't need your company. And target it. Think about what your customers would find useful, something they couldn't find easily themselves. Information is the easiest and most popular free offer to make. But other good ones are free consultations, free trials of goods and free samples.

Fig. 24. This is a confectionery-sales web site called Jelly Belly. It is using jelly beans as the basis of a free online offer.

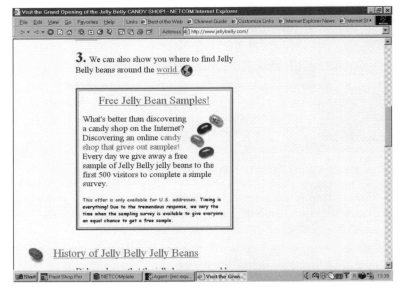

8. **Articles** about any subject related to your business are another winner. Make them informative, funny, well written and entertaining and update them regularly. Either get a writer to do you a regular series, or invite your visitors to send them in.

9. **Columns**. Everyone enjoys reading and then totally disagreeing with someone else's opinion, so columns are a great content provider. Have 'celebrity' columns on your site, using well-known people in your industry, or ask your visitors to write a column for you.

10 **Cartoons**. Another content winner and rarely used on business sites. No matter how serious your business, there's always a funny side to it. There are plenty of cartoonists who can create a page of cartoons for your site, and they're very popular with visitors.

11. **News**. A news service on your site will almost guarantee you plenty of regular visitors, especially if that news is updated daily or weekly. This can be a bit of an organisational headache, but visitors love catching up on industry headlines, so it can make your site stand out from others.

12. **Ordering information**. This is the important bit. Make it easy to read, understand, and fill in. Give lots of ways you can be contacted,

such as phone, fax and so on. And put your prices in several currencies − the internet is global, remember? Make ordering simple and easy, even if that does create problems for you. Customers will love you for it.

Question and answer

Where can we find all this information for our site?

A lot of it can be created by your own staff, and your content writer. There are companies on the internet that can keep your content up to date for you, if you feel you don't have the time to do it yourself.

How to overcome customer 'information fatigue'

All this information is great, but the trouble is that the internet is full of information − and this can lead to 'information fatigue' amongst your customers. Few companies bother to tackle it. By doing so, you give yourself another competitive advantage.

Information fatigue' is the point at which your visitor's brain simply says 'that's it, I'm out of here' as soon as it sees them hit another hyperlink on the screen. No matter how interesting and useful your content is, you could find that your visitor's brain isn't interested. But fear not, there is a solution. Turn your content into so-called 'eye candy' − a sort of Mars Bar for the brain. That doesn't mean you have to cover it in chocolate or use lots of colours. Instead make it interesting, and lay it out in a way that the brain can follow.

You may have heard of 'mind maps', popularised by Tony Buzan. If you haven't, I suggest you read his superb book *The Mind Map Book*. Though it would be difficult to read text laid out as a mind map, you can

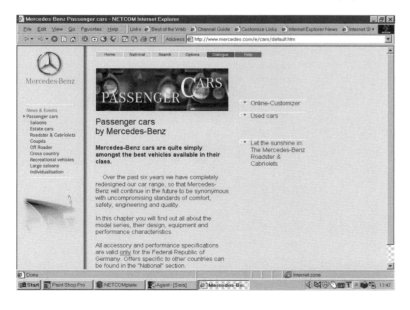

Fig. 25. Mercedes is an example of a well-known motor vehicle brand which is establishing itself successfully on the internet.

lay your content out according to mind map rules, which makes it easier to navigate, but complicated to put together. But since you're talking in a language the brain understands, your reader will understand your message quicker, and that is more likely to result in a sale.

Be warned! This is not something you should try at home, or even at work. You need the skills of a professional writer and preferably one who understands mind-mapping.

If all this sounds too complicated, then follow a few tried and tested ideas:

1. Keep your text short. Say what you want to say, in a brief, interesting and if possible funny way. And then stop.

2. Put plenty of white space around your text, and use a light-coloured background. Try to make your text fit nicely onto one screen. Link your sentences from one paragraph to the next . . .

3. Keep your reader interested. Treat topics in a different way, such as having an agony aunt column, cartoons, even soap operas. Make it interesting! Find unusual ways of presenting information, but not so unusual that it puts more conservative customers off.

Fig. 26. Edith Roman Online. This site is a great example of ways of attracting and keeping visitors. It has a free catalogue, downloads and calculators.

Sound complicated? It isn't really, but the rewards for making the effort speak for themselves. And not just in sales and sales leads, but also in terms of publicity.

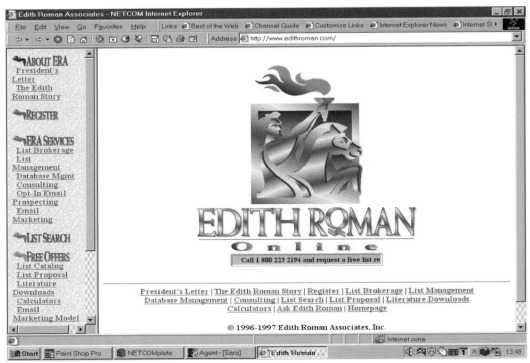

Question and answer

This all sounds a bit much for us. Is there anyone who could do this for us?

Indeed there is. If you're finding this approach tough going, then the services of a writer/editor with some design experience will be invaluable. Check out the search engines on the internet, or post a message into one of the newsgroups to find one.

Publicity-friendly content tactics

The internet is the one thing the media love most, after politicians who get involved in sex scandals. And they love anything about the internet that is a bit unusual. So any item that fits that criterion tends to get a lot of nice, free publicity, often in national newspapers. Sound good to you? It's not difficult to achieve, you just need to think a bit differently from everyone else.

We've looked at agony columns as a content idea, but they can also be a great way to get publicity for your site. Few sites have them, and if your site is on a subject that isn't really associated with agony aunts, you're on to a winner.

Here are a few other ideas:

1. **Soap operas** are another good publicity-getter. I know of a chemical company which asked their copywriter to create a soap opera that used the staff of the company. It went out in weekly episodes on their web site, and was a huge success, generating both publicity and profits.

2. A **controversial column** once a week or month for your web site. The media love controversy, and by taking an unusual stance on an industry subject you'll get plenty of publicity for your site as people rush to see what you've said – more so if you offer them a forum to reply in. You can find out a lot about your customers this way.

3. Take a **mundane subject** and talk about it in an **unusual way**. For instance, I helped a thermostat company to sell their thermostats via their web site. Instead of information about how great they were, I created two interactive articles with a sexy theme. There was one for women to read, and one for men. The thermostat featured in both pieces, as a sort of 'control your sex life' device. It worked very well, with the site getting plenty of publicity and thermostat sales rising nicely as a result.

There are plenty of other ideas; just be different or unusual in your approach, and then tell the media about it. If you can find a sexy angle, all the better. But you don't need to use sex as a selling point, anything will do, as long as it grabs the reader's curiosity. Make sure that whatever you do is relevant to your industry, your company and your site.

Generating quality leads online...

Question and answer

We'd like the publicity for our site, but we're nervous about using these approaches. Isn't there a danger we could alienate our customers?

Possibly. But then again, you know your customers best, and you know what would upset them. The bottom line is that the internet is big and is bordering on the huge. If you want your site to get the sales, then you have to be prepared to stand out from the crowd. That doesn't mean going to extremes, it means being a bit different.

The secrets of securing qualified sales leads and sales from your web site

Lots of visitors is a great thing, but are they the right visitors? Do they have the necessary buying power to buy your product or service? Good question, but one that can be answered without having to resort to time-consuming follow-up calls.

The internet is the perfect place to pre-qualify your sales leads and even your buyers. People are more willing to fill in forms and answer questions than if you write to them or phone them. You can use your special offer (you have sorted one out, haven't you?) as a way of sorting out the nerds from customers. On your special offers page, or ordering page, you put a simple form with, say, five questions. Any more than five questions and people tend to nod off while they're answering them.

Make your questions ones that need simple yes/no answers and give them a box to click, rather than asking them to type in Yes or No. How you ask the questions is very important. For instance, if you have a question that says:

> *'Would you be interested in buying our product/service?'*

you're inviting a yes, regardless of whether they have any real intention of doing so. But change that to:

> *'Have you bought a similar product or service recently?'*

and you'll get a more truthful answer. Don't ask me why, you just do. If you want to be really sneaky, ask who it was they bought from, and don't give them a list to choose from. The questions you use will depend on your company and industry. But a few general ones you could use are:

1. Do you have any problems with your whatsit (whatsit being whatever product or service you supply)? Underneath it show a list of possible problems they might have which they can choose from.

2. Will you have a need for our product/service within the next six months/year/century/generation of family? Put in whichever suits you.

3. Do you believe that your company would profit from our whatsit solution?

People who go to the trouble of filling in these forms are likely to be interested prospects and ones with the necessaries to buy. By using the form and a specially targeted offer you can weed out the wannabe buyer from the serious buyer. When they send in the information, jump to it. The sooner you get your offer to them, the more likely they are to buy. Too many companies don't take their email seriously enough, as you'll discover.

Question and answer

Isn't there a risk that some of our potential customers won't want to go to the bother of filling out a form, and therefore we risk losing a sale?

Maybe. But you can get round this by putting your phone, fax and email at the top of the form and explaining that the visitor can contact you that way instead.

Case studies

The boss's blunder
Charles runs a medium-sized company and has decided to put an email contact address on their web site, so that potential customers can contact their salesman, Andrew, with any questions. Andrew doesn't really understand how to use the company's email account, so he sends back a form message to anyone who writes, telling them to phone instead. As a result, the company loses three major new accounts to its competitor.

Healing a web site
Angela is in charge of her Health Trust's web site, which isn't doing as well as they would like. So far, all they've had is a lot of junk mail to their email address. Angela gets in touch with patients who visit their site, and finds out that many of them would like a 'real' person to reply to their emails. She decides to do this herself, asking the doctors to reply to any queries she can't answer. It's a great success, and results in the web site being visited more than ever, and the Health Trust winning an award.

5 Attracting visitors to your web site

In this chapter we will explore:

▶ *usenet, content services, links, search engines and PR*

▶ *a few little-known tactics you can use to get more visitors*

▶ *what kind of offers attract which kind of prospects*

▶ *how to attract the prospects you want to visit your site.*

. . . .

How to use usenet, content services, links, search engines and PR

'Build and they will come' is a statement that many companies take to heart when it comes to their web site. If it was true, then all you'd need to do is put your site online and off you go. In the early days of the web, there were so few sites that people did visit them out of curiosity, but now you have to attract them to your site.

One of the most important concepts to understand is that you need the right sort of people visiting your site – quality of hits, rather than quantity. This is especially important if you intend selling ad space to others. There are five basic ways to help your visitors find out about your site, and we'll look at each one in detail. The first is usenet.

Usenet

Usenet is a large group of bulletin boards, covering all sorts of subjects. Each board is called a **newsgroup**, and allows anyone to post a message which others can read and respond to. Find the groups that are related to your business area. You'll be surprised how many there are. Then read them for a week or so, follow some of the messages' subject matter, and watch to see how others promote their services and products.

The most successful of these companies write messages that no one can take offence at. Let's say you're a computer consulting company specialising in wide area networks. Someone has asked about a software problem they are having. You could answer giving the person some information about how to solve the problem, and if they would like more help to get in touch with you via private email.

You would also have a **signature line**, or sig line, which is a couple of sentences underneath where you put your name at the end of a message. Some people think big is best, and have huge sig lines. But less is very much more on usenet. You could use your USP (unique sales point) or your positioning statement, together with your web site address.

One of the most successful messages we have seen in a long time, and one which the company concerned uses again and again, is to help someone who they think may be doing business with their competitor. They post in a message saying something like this:

> *'though we ourselves wouldn't recommend using that piece of software, because of the problems you're suffering, why not trying doing this to sort the problem out...'*

and then go on to detail that help.

Those messages have generated thousands of hits from usenet, and some valuable sales as well.

Another way you can encourage people to visit your site is to **post** in a short article, or five tips for something, with just your sig line with it. People rarely object to useful information that is posted in, providing there's no blatant plugging of the company concerned.

Fig. 27. Viewing messages in a newsgroup. The newsgroups are shown on the left, and the messages in the highlighted news-group are shown on the right. Click on a message header to read a message; for example, the messages on Getting Leads (highlighted).

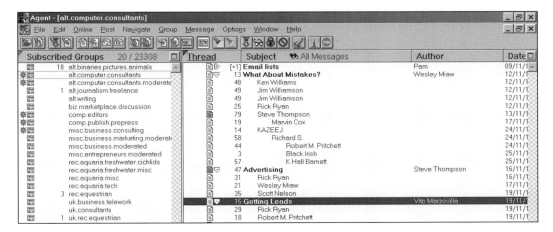

All this of course is time-consuming, and you may find that you would prefer a company to do this for you. The rewards, though, are excellent. A lot more people **lurk** – that is, read but don't post into these groups – and they often visit a site to find out more. So, if you want to use usenet to help market your site and company:

▷ Discover which newsgroups are read by your market.

▷ Read them yourself for a week or so, to get the gist of things.

▷ Avoid posting in commercial messages.

▷ Answer questions that you can in a helpful friendly way.

▷ Organise a simple but effective sig line. A copywriter can help you with this.

▷ Post in helpful information for other users of the group.

▷ Avoid getting into 'flame' wars or arguments online.

▷ Work to get your company perceived as the best company for that area.

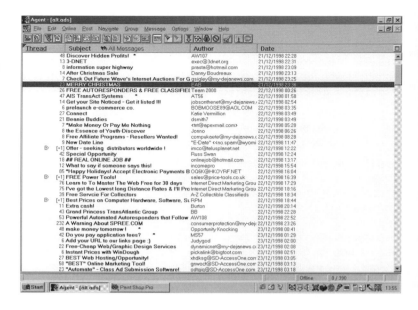

Fig. 28. This is a newsgroup called 'alt.ads'. Each line shows the message header, the name of the person who posted the message, and the date it was posted. Highlight and click on any line to read the message.

Content services

Content services and sites are another fertile hunting ground. Content services are provided by companies such as:

> AOL (America Online)
> CompuServe
> MSN (MicroSoft Network)

These services have areas where only their members can post messages. Most of these services are American-dominated, but this is changing, and they tend to be full of more professional people. You will need to subscribe to these services to be able to use them. Most offer a free 30-day trial, so it's worth taking them up on it, to make sure that the service has something you need. These services also have commercial areas where you can put ads and the like, without the risk of been flamed.

Fig. 29. America Online (AOL) has been hugely successful in attracting visitors to its web site. Using many enticing features, it has persuaded more than 20 million people world wide to take out subscriptions.

You'll find a huge mixture of groups similar to usenet. Many of these services also have special areas dedicated to a particular subject, which can be helpful for targeting your market. You may also be able to purchase advertising space in these areas.

The same rules apply here as on usenet. Be careful what you say and what you post, and try to be helpful, friendly and polite. Some of these services don't allow sig lines, as part of their rules. But there is a way round this. Instead of using your sig line, invite people to get in touch with you at your email address. Many will do so, as their software will allow them to click on your address and send you a message.

Tips on using the content services

If you want to use the content services:

1. Take up any free trials they are offering to check they have areas which are useful to you.
2. Note that people on these services tend to be more friendly and professional than on usenet.
3. If you get stuck, email the **sysop** of the forum or group you're trying to use. The sysop (systems operator) is the group's manager and will be glad to help you out.
4. Many of these services have file areas, where you can put reports, articles and so on for people to download. Take advantage of this.
5. You might find it a good idea to buy advertising space in areas dedicated to your subject.
6. Offer to do a conference or live talk. These are very popular and only require an hour or so of your time. They help build your reputation as someone who knows what they're talking about.

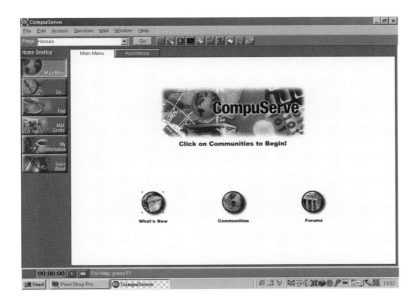

Fig. 30. CompuServe has been very successful in using the marketing concept of 'community' to attract visitors and subscribers to its content-packed site.

Content sites and search engines ....

Content sites

Content sites are slightly different from the content services. These sites exist on the web. Some are ones where you must register to get access, others charge, and others are free. They all feature a specific subject such as computer networking, insurance, commercial finance and so on. They often have online forums you can post into, message areas, etc. However, do check the rules for each one before posting anything in.

These sites are always keen to take material and content that is relevant to their readers, so you could find yourself with a lucrative outlet for bringing people to your site, by offering them articles, features and reports.

If you want to use these sites, here are a few tips:

(a) Have a good look round and a good read of the site.

(b) Ask the owner about who visits the site.

(c) Ask the owner if they are willing to take material from you in return for a link. If yes, then offer them reports, articles, features, columns – anything that their readers would like.

(d) Offer to set up a conference or online seminar at the site free of charge.

Search engines

Search engines are probably the way most people find a web site. There are more and more of them appearing each year, and to make matters worse for marketers, each one has different criteria for accepting sites.

Yahoo! is the most well known, and also the toughest to get onto. Each site is reviewed by real people, rather than checked by a machine. Other big search engines include HotBot, SearchUK, AltaVista and Infoseek.

Fig. 31. Yahoo! is the most used internet directory and search engine on the planet. Do everything possible to make sure you are listed here.

56

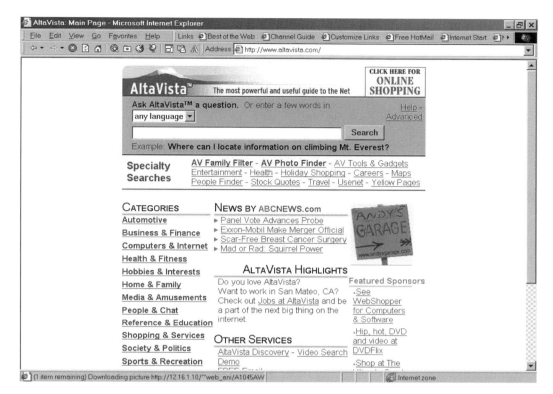

Fig. 32. AltaVista is one of the top ten internet search engines and databases. It will really pay to get your site listed here.

There are companies who you can pay to get you a good ranking on the search engine. Basically, the nearer you come to the top of the user's search, the better your chances of your site getting visited. You could literally spend all of your time maintaining your ranking, so unless you feel it is absolutely worth it, don't bother too much about it.

Here are a few ways you can improve your ranking:

▷ Change your content regularly.

▷ Use 'meta-tags' in your HTML code. Your designer can do this for you.

▷ Make sure certain keywords about your business are on the first web page, such as your company name, and business subject area.

▷ Give each page a title that reflects your business.

▷ Make sure your pages don't take an age to load up.

Also, don't ignore the many country-specific search engines and other search engines that are dedicated to your business area. These can be better bets than the major engines.

Links

These are the cornerstone of many a web marketer's campaign. Links should really work to get people to your site, rather than away from it. You can get round this by using frames on your site, though this won't make you popular with some people. This way, the visitor never really leaves your site, whereas if you link away from your site, they may well not come back.

Here are a few linking tips:

1. Get in touch with sites covering your area of business and ask to be put on their link site. But don't at first offer a link back to their site. Only agree to this if the site is one you feel is not in direct competition with you.

2. Many online e-zines and newsletters publish new links each month, so submit yours to the relevant publications.

3. Try offline magazines which have web sites – they often let you link to them.

4. Get a link from your trade association's site, and from foreign organisations that fill a similar role.

5. Avoid giving a link back to the linker's site, if at all possible.

Public relations

PR online is rapidly developing into an industry in itself. If you prefer to have an agency do it for you, then you have that choice. Getting good PR is as tough online as it is offline.

Successful PR requires some lateral thinking, and the willingness to stick your neck out. But the rewards can be excellent. Many companies have found that their online PR has led to offline PR which they don't have to pay for. The knack is to be newsworthy, and applicable to your target market. Here are a few tried and tested ideas:

1. Get an interview with someone famous or well respected and put it on your site. And then contact other sites, e-zines and so on.

2. Put some innovative new idea on your site. The Halifax bank did this with their mortgage calculator.

3. Offer a special report, with some exclusive information in it.

4. Make a special offer. The first 50 people to do something, get this.

5. Sponsor a site which deals with a good cause, preferably one related to your company's subject area.

6. Win a web award for your site.

7. Run a competition with excellent prizes.

8. One company held an auction of its staff's expertise. The staff would go and help whoever bid the most for a day. The money raised was donated to charity.

9. Offer something on your site that has never been offered or seen before. NASA have done this with their photos from the Hubble telescope.

Question and answer

My company wants a quick and effective way of getting more visitors to our site. All these seem too time-consuming – what else could I try?

Marketing online is similar to marketing in the real world in this case. Odd things may bring huge amounts of visitors to your site, such as your frying pan having been used on a Delia Smith TV programme which dramatically boosts sales around the world. The hard truth is that marketing online takes time and persistence.

A few little-known tactics you can use to get more visitors

Here are a few tactics our business has used with various companies and which have been successful.

▷ *Company A* – had their writer produce a special report, detailing the successful marketing methods of their clients' competitors. The report was widely publicised to their target audience, and you could only get a copy by filling out a form on their site. The site was carefully organised so that the visitor was led through relevant product information before they could register for the report. The result was a 200 per cent increase in visitors, and a 75 per cent increase in sales.

▷ *Company B* – complained to one of the large search engines that one of their competitors was using a lot of irrelevant keywords and meta-tag description on their web site. The competitor's site was ranked 20 places above Company B's. The competitor was removed from that search engine and three others, and Company B's site was now ranked third.

▷ *Company C* – created a controversial column for their site, which was heavily marketed to target magazines, newspapers and their customers and potential customers. The site was mentioned in nearly every trade magazine and newspaper covering their industry sector, and resulted in a 300 per cent jump in visitors – and a very respectable increase in sales.

▷ *Company D* – asked us to keep an eye on a competitor's site and marketing tactics. We discovered several areas where they were the only company in their sector using that particular media to advertise their site. Company D then blitzed this and other related areas themselves, and increased hits by 200 per cent and sales by 40 per cent.

▷ *Company E* – offered to host their leading trade magazine on their site. The magazine, which until then had no web presence, agreed. The experiment was a great success. When the magazine built its own web site, it made sure Company E got a prominent link. This link has brought in an extra 22,000 visitors each month.

Question and answer

This makes it sound like I have to be constantly 'on the ball' to spot these opportunities. What if I don't have the time to do this kind of thing?

The internet is an ever-changing technology, so staying 'on the ball' is vital. If you find this daunting, there are companies who can do most of the work for you, though you will have to pay for the privilege.

What kind of offers attract what kind of prospects?

The kind of offer you make on your site will determine what kind of prospects you have getting in touch with you. There are as many types of offer as there are prospects, but here are a few pointers to what attracts whom:

1. Free information is always popular, and tends to attract everyone, from the serious buyer to the just interested. The more valuable and targeted the information you're offering, the more likely you are to get serious potential customers.

2. Software is another popular option, though again it must be carefully targeted or you'll end up with the wrong kind of prospects visiting your site. A person who downloads trial software is often a serious buyer, though they may just be a trier.

3. Free consultations and so on, if these are offered on the site as it is, are likely to attract a relatively low level of good prospects. Many people go for every freebie they can find, whether it is relevant to them or not. Only allow registered users of your site to qualify for your free consultation, as they're serious enough about it to go to the trouble of registering.

4. Free catalogues and other information create a lot of 'just warm' prospects. Unless you ask them to fill in a form they could easily be just catalogue collectors rather than serious prospects for your company

If you're unsure what to offer, ask your customers. They have been serious enough in the past to buy from you, so ask what would attract them. This is very seldom done, but makes a huge amount of difference to the commercial success of your site.

How to get the prospects you want to visit your site

As has been mentioned before, you need quality visitors, rather than a quantity of visitors. To find them you need to look at your target market, find the sub-segments that make it up, and then tie these in with your niches online. Many companies worry that their competitors could steal their visitors, and that visitors have no loyalty to a site. Most visitors are very loyal to sites they like and which continue to provide content that meets their needs. As for competitors stealing your visitors, it's unlikely that you will all have exactly the same niche and sub-segments of that niche.

To get the right kind of prospects coming to your site, you first have to find where they are at the moment:

(a) Which mailing lists do they read?

(b) Which newsletters?

(c) Which sites do they visit most?

You need to almost move in with your potential prospects online. The more you know about them, the better your chances of getting them to your site.

Guidelines for attracting the right kind of prospects

▷ Define exactly who you are looking for.

▷ Find out as much about their online activity as you can.

▷ Read what they read, visit the sites they do and see what areas seem the most popular.

▷ Try and find out which mediums they respond best to. Banner ads? Links? Information-based links?

▷ Make them offers that they are known to like and respond to.

▷ Find out what they don't like and make sure you don't do anything they hate.

▷ Find out what their problems are.

▷ Market your site according to the information you discover.

▷ Be specific. Using such and such magazine as a means of attracting prospects is great, but only if its readers are the people you want. Go for quality of readers rather than quantity.

The important point here is not to think of the internet as 30 million possible customers, because in fact there are not 30 million customers who all want what you sell online. Nevertheless, there are hundreds of thousands of profitable niches and sub-segments which are hardly being exploited. It's like everyone mining near the top of a hill for some gold, when three feet further down there's tons of the stuff.

Getting visitors to your web site is one thing, keeping them coming back is another. Have no fear, the next chapter will explain how you can keep yours loyal to your site.

Case studies ....

Question and answer

Could I use existing information I know about my customers, to help attract the right kind of prospects to my site?

Of course! But do make sure you find out from them what their internet preferences are. These can often be different from their offline preferences. You may find that an offer you make in the real world can easily translate into a popular offer online.

Case studies

Linda gets linked
Linda has found there are 15 sites which are directly relevant to her business. All of them have a high proportion of the type of prospects she wants. She asks at all the sites if she can have a link from their site in return for a popular regular column she writes.

The site owners all agree, but only if they get a link back. Linda is desperate for visitors and agrees. To her dismay, she finds she's only getting 'quick hits', people who visit the site for a minute or so and then go away. She soon finds out why: the other sites are using 'aggressive framing' so when the visitor clicks to her site, the previous site's frames dominate most of the screen, making her site look small, and cutting off most of her front page. No wonder no one stays for long!

Polly gets her prospects right
Polly has limited funds and needs to make her web site pay for itself quickly. She spends several weeks of her spare time finding out as much as she can about her potential customers' likes and dislikes.

She asks hundreds of people for help and advice, and builds an impressive dossier of information. She then changes her site to accommodate the new information and changes her offers and freebies. With some blitz-like marketing she finds that, despite a relatively low hit count, she is making a sale from every third visitor!

6 Keeping your customers coming back

In this chapter we will explore:

▶ *making your visitors an offer they can't refuse – what works and what doesn't*

▶ *building visitor loyalty*

▶ *keeping your site regularly updated, and with what*

▶ *secrets that the most popular sites on the net use, and how you can use them too.*

. . . .

Making your visitors an offer they can't refuse – what works and what doesn't

We talked about offers in the last chapter, but if you want your visitors to turn into regulars, then you need to get them to register at your site. Registration is one area of internet marketing that more companies slip up on than any other. You've probably come across registration at sites you've visited – you're asked to fill in details about yourself and maybe your likes and dislikes.

Many visitors hate registration forms, not because they resent filling them in, but because they resent spending their time and money filling them in and not getting much in return. Promises such as 'this helps us tune our site to your needs' just don't wash any more. Visitors are aware that their data is valuable to you, so they want something more than promises.

Generally, the more data you want from them, the more you're going to have to give them in return. Here are a few items that other companies have successfully used on their sites:

1. cash offers

2. discounts on products or services

3. subscriptions to publications

4. entitlement to a valuable 'freebie'

5. exclusive information

6. relevant gifts

7. personalised information.

If you decide not to offer anything to people who register, then you may find your registrations aren't as good as you would like them to be. The

Collecting customer information online ....

same applies if you offer something that your visitors don't perceive as valuable. Here are a few items that are now considered 'boring' or just not worth bothering with online:

1. information which can be easily found elsewhere

2. subscription to company newsletters that are nothing more than PR

3. gifts that never arrive

4. tacky gifts

5. very small discounts (most people expect at least 10 per cent off)

6. free trials of goods or services which aren't really free trials.

There are various protection laws for data collected online, so it's important to remember that any data you do collect is subject to the same laws as the data you collect offline. It's also vital that you include a tick box on your registration form, for visitors to tick if they do not wish to get further information from you (though you could 'bribe' them not to tick it, by offering extra goodies if they don't). Many people leave these boxes blank, in the hope that you'll send them some good offers anyway.

Whatever offer you make, be sure that you can go through with it. Your site could be very successful and leave you with no time to do the paying work you should be doing, if you've offered free consultations. Be prepared for a lot of responses, or not many at all. The key is to get *quality* responses. To get those you need to:

1. make offers your visitors want

2. follow up with the offer

3. treat the person as you would a paying client

4. make your form as short but as detailed as possible.

Here are a few fields you could have on your form to help you get the quality of responses you want:

(a) name, company name, and company address

(b) phone, fax, email and so on

(c) title of the person's job within the company (d) what responsibilities they have

(e) number of employees

(f) whether they have bought your type of product or service before

(g) any problems they are having which are related to your area of work.

The trick is to ask questions that don't require a yes or no answer, and then to give the visitor the choice of several options as an answer. This

Horse Magazine - Equiworld Horse Magazine - Microsoft Internet Explorer

File   Edit   View   Go   Favorites   Help | Links Best of the Web   Channel Guide   Customize Links   Free HotMail   Internet Start

equiworld.net

Your Own Equestrian Resource!

July 1997
World Issue

[Previous Issue]   [Issue Index]   [Next Issue]

Contents

Finding Riding Holidays?

Who Draws Mr Ned?

New Look
Welcome to the new look Equiworld. We hope you enjoy the new the new format.

Books
Your guide to equestrian books. Including details of where to buy Laura Collins "A Career in the Horse Industry". Also included links to the Equiworld books directory.

British Breeds
Trying to find out more about your horse breeds, this issue brings you a directory of British Horse Breed Organisations.

Live Chat
Find out more about using the internet to chat about horsey things. This month we provide links to hot chat systems, with hints and tips.

Classifieds

Start | Horse Magazine | Paint Shop Pro   13:50

---

way you get a more accurate answer, than a yes or no. One company rather infamously asked its visitors if their sales were good. Since it only offered yes or no as an option they didn't find out very much.

Test your offers with visitors to see which is the most popular. This is a bit time-consuming, but when you've found out which your visitors like best, then you can use it without any worries. What you offer will decide whether your visitors register with you or not. So go to the trouble of finding out what they would like and how they would like it. And if you're stuck, then the question below might help.

Question and aswer

We make an offer of a free consultation in our offline marketing, but this would be impossible to implement for overseas visitors. What else could we offer?

Why not take the most commonly asked questions in your consultation and write them into an interactive report which could be emailed or sent on disk? The visitor could then work their way through it and email the results back to you for analysis.

Building customer loyalty

Now you've got people coming to your site, and they are registering with your site, you need to keep them coming back to your site. Visitors tend to be loyal to sites they like best, often bookmarking or 'off-portalling' the

Fig. 33. Equiworld is an example of a web site designed to keep its customers coming back. Its New Look, Live Chat, and Classified sections, for example, are all likely to offer fresh and up-to-date content.

site. A bookmark is a link which is saved in your browser as, say, a favourite location.

Off-portalling is a new concept, developed from so-called **portal** sites. Portal sites aim to be the site your browser defaults to. In many cases this is your internet service provider's home page or the Microsoft or Netscape home page.

Search engines such as Yahoo! have been developing themselves into portal sites, in the hope of attracting more visitors and large advertising revenues. Off-portalling is similar, but here the user keeps their favourite site in their browser's cache. This way, when they go online they can quickly get to the area of the site they want, without waiting for it to load.

Getting people to use your site as their bookmark is relatively easy, as is off-portalling since many people do this anyway. But getting them to make your site the portal site for their browser is more difficult, as it requires the user to go into their browser's settings and change them. Although this is simple to do, many people are nervous of altering them.

There are many ways you can build customer and visitor loyalty to your site. Here are a few of them:

▷ Keep your site up to date with relevant information.

▷ Use personalisation for your registered users.

▷ Have interactive elements and forums on your site.

▷ Get back to customer queries as quickly as possible.

▷ Answer complaints quickly.

▷ Thank people for bothering to write and comment on your site, even if it is negative.

▷ Find out what your visitors want and then give it to them.

These are just a few basic ways in which you can encourage loyalty from your visitors. The most important of these is keeping up-to-date, relevant information on your site, which your visitors are interested in and want to read. You could ask your readers to vote on their favourite and least favourite areas of the site, to help you find out what they value most.

As a rule, people stay loyal to a site that helps solve their problems. They like a site that gives them the feeling they are part of a special community, a company that is seen to care about them and their needs, a site that understands what is expected of them in their job, or in their business. They also value information that helps them to do their job better and makes them stand out in the corporate structure.

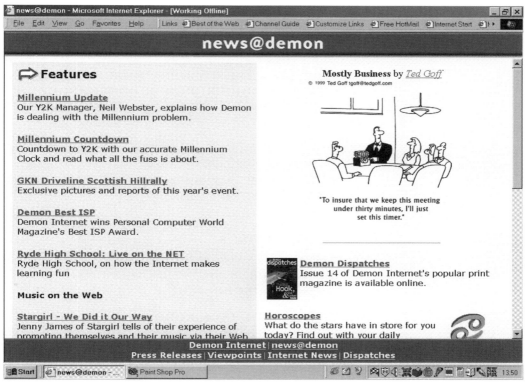

We covered content in a previous chapter, so here are a few areas which you need to keep up to date if you're going to keep your visitors loyal to your site:

Fig. 34. Demon Internet was the first UK internet service provider to score a big hit. Its site is packed with ever-changing features and content to keep people coming back.

▷ news
▷ articles
▷ columns
▷ features
▷ question and answer pages
▷ any interactive elements you have
▷ prices, if you have them online
▷ product information
▷ frequently asked question sheets.

If your site is seen to be constantly updated, then your visitors will value it more. Here are a few extra items that you might find useful to have on your site:

▷ reports on shows, exhibitions and conferences
▷ new developments in your field and what they mean for your customers
▷ new techniques that can make or save them money and/or time
▷ reports
▷ interviews with people within your industry
▷ information about national issues and how your customers can exploit them.

The importance of being up to date......................................

You can probably see a pattern here. All the information is geared to helping your customer or visitor. Visitors are interested in you, but they are also much more interested in themselves and their problems. The knack is to subtly sell yourself as the solution to their problems in everything you do on your site. It isn't easy to achieve, but when it's done well, it works.

Another important point is that you need to have a consistent feel to your site. Add new things by all means, but keep them consistent with the message and feel you want to get across to your visitors. Lack of consistency is one reason why so many people stop visiting a site on a regular basis.

Question and answer

I felt that when we had built the web site and marketed it, that would be that. I was only looking to update our site if something new happened. Do I really need to update it more than that?

Yes! Few people enjoy reading the same things over and over again. No matter how brilliant your site is, its content ages very quickly online, far quicker than, say, in an offline newsletter.

This is why, if you're serious about marketing online, you must schedule in the time to keep the site bang up to date.

Keeping your site regularly updated and with what

We looked at a few items above that you need to keep updated on your site. Now we'll look at those in a bit more detail.

News

Magazines may be able to get away with news that isn't up-to-the-minute but web sites can't. People are used to being able to read news as it happens, getting stock market quotes and so on. The internet is an 'instant' culture, so your news needs to be kept up to date.

If this isn't possible, there are ways round it.

You could buy in a relevant **news feed** from an organisation and use that on your site. Or you could have a 'behind the news' area on your site. These are popular with visitors. Here you'd look at news items that affect your industry, such as mergers, new legislation and so on, but instead of saying 'so-and-so took over what-not' you look at the implications of it for your industry.

This approach really needs the hand of your content writer. News writing is an art, and when it's done right it is popular with visitors.

Articles, features and columns

There's a real lack of decent quality articles, features and columns for various industries online. While online journalism – especially consumer journalism – has taken off, there's been little movement in the various business sectors. This is excellent news for you.
The most popular types of articles are:

1. how we/I did it

2. how to

3. behind the scenes/looks at various aspects of your industry

4. how to make the most of new legislation, mergers and so on

5. personal experience.

Anything that helps, educates or solves a problem will be popular with your visitor.

▷ Warning – Some sites haven't been able to resist the temptation to 'borrow' articles from their leading trade magazine. This is a breach of copyright, and can be very expensive if you're caught out. Many companies believe they can get away with it, because of the sheer mass of information on the net. But many publishing houses now employ people to keep an eye on their material, and make sure none is used without their permission.

Apart from anything else, plagiarism makes your site look bad anyway. Maybe one of your staff could write the material; if not, you could find a friendly journalist (they do exist!) to write the material for you. There are also many excellent freelance writers who specialise in particular industries who may be able to help you.

Columns are another favourite of visitors, especially controversial ones, where the visitor can put a reply in a forum. If you can find someone in your company who can write well, and has a bit of an inside edge on your sector, then they would make an excellent columnist. Or you could approach a columnist in an industry magazine and ask them to write for your site.

Question and answer pages

These are always popular on web sites. There are several approaches you can adopt:

▷ *Frequently asked questions (FAQs)* – These could cover your company, your products and services, or aspects of your industry. Keeping these up to date is important, otherwise your visitor might try and use inaccurate information, which could have serious repercussions for you.

▷ *Question and answer pages* – These aren't used as often as they could be. Many people don't like reading on their computer screen, so making these downloadable and readable offline will be a major plus for your site.

▷ *Question and answer sheets* – These could cover all sorts: legislation, new products coming on the market, making more of existing products, how to do a particular thing with an existing product. The list is almost endless.

PRODUCT INFORMATION

People love to know more about what they're thinking of buying, and the more expensive it is, the more they want to know about it.

Many companies simply scan in catalogues, brochures, information sheets and so on and put those online. But this is a mistake.

The web is interactive, and a static document seems a waste when you could do so much more. As a result many companies now offer CDs with a presentation about their material. Others offer downloadable material, such as:

> presentations
> video clips
> word-processor files containing photographs.

Some even give over a whole section of their site to their products and what they can do. For example, you could lead your visitor through a set of questions to find out which product suits them best, and then take them to that area of the site. Offer them an 'all-singing, all-dancing' video clips option, or text and pictures that can be downloaded.

Another method being successfully used is to allow the customer to 'build' the product they want online, and then give them a quote. There is an amazing range of possibilities when you start to think in terms of interactivity, rather than just a static document. And it will make your site stand out, over all the others.

So how often should you update your site? This depends on your business and your product's life cycle. Ideally you should be updating once a week. But most companies prefer to go for once a month.

If you feel that this is going to be too time-consuming, you could outsource the work to another company who can take over the content generation and updating the site needs. All the work they do should be approved by you before it goes online. They will work with either their own writers or specialists to produce high quality material. The drawback is that it isn't cheap, but if you can't spare the personnel, then this could be the cheaper option in the long run. Here are a few pointers for choosing a company for doing this work:

1. Ask how long they have been doing this kind of work.

2. Do they understand your industry?

3. Are they specialists or generalists?

4. Are their writers professionals?

5. Will they be responsible for the coding of the material?

6. Will they upload the material for you?

7. Are they responsible for the copyright of the material they produce?

Site maintenance is the most easily ignored of all aspects of internet marketing. It's time-consuming, can be difficult, and often requires outside professional help. The beauty of doing it is that few sites do it well, so when you do, you automatically rise above the rest.

Question and answer

Is there any way we can keep our site's content maintained on a tight budget?

Of course. If you're willing to take on the task of writing, coding and uploading the material yourself you can save a lot of money. Or you could buy in syndicated columns or features from a syndication agency. Ask your visitors to contribute material in return for a plug for their company. There are plenty of ideas.

Secrets that the most popular sites on the net use, and how you can use them too

So how do the most popular sites on the net keep their sites updated? Do they have huge budgets? Teams of staff dedicated to their sites? Not in all cases. Most of these sites started on quite limited budgets, where necessity was the mother of invention. Here are a few ideas they use that you can use on your site:

1. Encourage your visitors to send you articles, features and so on.

2. Get in touch with journalists in your field, and ask if you can buy First Electronic Rights in some of their already published work.

3. Offer publishers ad space and plugs on your site in return for a sample chapter and author interview.

4, Put archived articles, features and materials in a registered-visitors- only section of your site. This way you get more registrations, and you can find out which are the most popular articles you've run.

5. Search out interesting people in your industry who aren't widely known and interview them for your site.

6. Get in touch with customers who are successfully using your products and interview them about how your product solved a problem they were having.

7. Have an online round-table discussion about a major trend in your industry.

8. Hold an online seminar.

9. Hold a competition.

10. Show alternative uses for your product, by asking customers to send them in.

11. Set aside a fixed time each month to update the site.

12. Devise a plan for which bits of the site are going to be updated and which aren't. You'd be amazed how many companies never do this.

These are just a few ideas. Finding content and keeping your site maintained on a budget isn't easy, but you can do it, with a bit of lateral thinking, so encourage your staff to make suggestions.

Another budget way of keeping your site maintained is to ask students looking for web experience to do it for you. Some big sites do this to keep costs down. If it's good enough for them . . .

Case studies

Clare courts disaster
Clare has been given the job of providing the content for her company web site. She's a good writer, and enjoys researching things and writing them up. Each month she creates some new material, using the company's external and internal newsletter, and other material she's created.
One month she reads a fascinating piece in a trade magazine, and decides to rewrite it slightly and put it on the site. The piece is a huge hit with visitors, and with the publication's lawyers who threaten legal action if the piece isn't removed immediately.

Brian's brainwave
Brian is no writer and he admits it. But his boss feels that he is the best person to maintain the company web site, because he knows so much about computers. Brian is at a total loss, he doesn't know what to do! He emails a freelance writer who writes for his trade magazine, and asks for some advice. The journalist sends him a huge message full of ideas, and contacts he knows who would be able to help. He also suggests contacting customers and suppliers for help. Brian soon finds that, although he still can't write really well, he can rewrite the material that he's now getting and puts it on the site. His boss is very happy and so are the site's visitors.

7 That's not all!
More ways you can market online

In this chapter we will explore the following in more detail:

▶ *usenet, forums, special interest groups, and how to use them successfully*

▶ *using direct email, without any nasty side-effects*

▶ *using online seminars and conferences to market your business*

▶ *5 unusual ways to market your business online.*

. . . .

Usenet, forums, special interest groups, and how to use them successfully

We looked at these in an earlier chapter, but now we'll go into more detail about how you can use them in an effective manner. To recap, you can use forums and so on:

1. to get visitors to your site

2. as part of a 'two-stage' selling process

3. to build your brand

4. as a relationship-builder with customers and potential customers

5. as a public relations vehicle.

The beauty of these groups is that in many cases you can do several of these things at once. Blatant commercial advertising is not acceptable in many groups and forums, though some do exist for the sole use of advertising. Responses from these tend to be low, as your message can easily get jostled out of place by the sheer number of ads posted every day.

Before you start to think about what you might want to post into these groups, your first task should be to make a list of the ones that you think your customers read. Better still, make a list of the ones you know from market research that your customers and potential customers read. You'll be able to see all the available usenet groups:

(a) from your service provider

(b) by visiting DejaNews at: www.dejanews.com.

DejaNews is a valuable and well-known resource for online marketing. It archives the messages posted into usenet groups, and allows you to do searches amongst them.

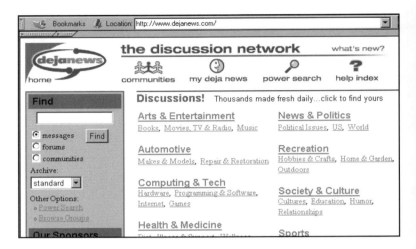

Fig. 35. DejaNews, the best-known searchable database of newsgroups and newsgroup messages.

Your next step is to do some lateral thinking. Consider which related groups your customers and potential customers may also be in. For instance, if you run a recruitment consultancy, your obvious target would be the jobs newsgroups. If you run an equestrian company, your obvious target would be the equestrian newsgroups.

A lot of horsey people also have dogs and cats, so the dogs and cats newsgroups would also make a good place to post into, as would groups dealing with various equestrian sports, clothing and so on. Many companies restrict themselves to their area of business and miss out on the huge opportunities in other newsgroups.

As we discussed before, your next step is to read these groups over a period of at least a week. In this way you will get a feel for the group and the people who post into it. Often there are a few people who regularly post into a group. If the group is moderated, it's a good idea to get in touch with the moderator, explain your intentions, and ask for any advice they can give you. Moderators appreciate companies who take the time to do this, and often tell you useful bits and pieces about the group that you wouldn't otherwise easily find out.

Your next step is to decide what your aim is in using these groups. Let's look at each in turn.

Getting visitors to your site

You can do this in two ways:

(a) the passive way, through your signature line

(b) the positive way, by posting a message which has something about your site in it. Here's an example: Signature line: 'Discover how to or-ganise your time more effectively in a special article written for our site www.xyz.net - XYZ Company, leaders in time management courses.'

With a message you could post part of the article into the group and make the remainder available on your site for the reader to read. It's tempting to ask people to email you back for the article. But this way they won't visit your site directly, which could lose you valuable sales.

The knack is not to post too little so it looks like a blatant push for your site, or too much so the reader has no reason to visit your site. Start your message with something like:

> 'We have an article on our site which we feel you would find useful, here's part of it...'

One of the best kept secrets of using usenet and forums is to 'get under' the readers of the group. By being friendly, polite, and even a little subservient to the group – which may have been around a long time – you make it difficult for others to get nasty about you, and you will make yourself look more 'caring' than other subscribers in the group. In most newsgroups there are subscribers who dislike any kind of commercialism and it's those people you have to watch.

So to use groups to get your site more visitors:

(a) understand how the group works

(b) be polite, understanding, friendly and even a little subservient

(c) post using your real name, and your company name

(d) have a short, to-the-point signature line

(e) look at related groups for your postings, but don't 'cross-post' messages.

Using newsgroups as part of a 'two-stage' selling process

This has become more difficult as the groups on the internet have developed, but you can still use it if you feel your product or service is easier to sell this way. Whatever you do, though, please don't take your direct mail letters, sales letters or whatever and post those into a group. Instead use one of two methods:

1. The first is to post in a message with the subject line 'Commercial message/your subject' or the like, and then have a polite, friendly message, giving the reader some interesting or valuable information and a contact for you, preferably an email one. Sending people direct to your web site just creates a perception that you're only interested in increasing your visitor figures. Your aim is to seem personal and professional. Personal attention counts for a lot online.

2. The second method you can use is when a **thread** starts about a problem that your product or service can solve. Post a helpful message, with a bit of information that can help people, and then say that you have a product or service that can help, requesting email for more details.

So to use these groups to 'two-stage' sell:

(a) Be polite, helpful and professional.

(b) Be careful about what you post into the group.

(c) Help people if you can.

(d) Don't post in your sales letters as they are, no matter how successful.

Building your brand and building a relationship with customers and potential customers

These two are pretty much the same thing, and can be approached in a similar way online. The important thing here is to be constantly and consistently helpful. These groups on the internet are used not just for general chat or passing on news but also for problem-solving and advice. They are a goldmine from a business point of view: lots of people all with problems you can help them solve, profitably. Whenever you see a message from someone with a problem, post in a helpful answer, as we discussed in an earlier chapter. By doing this consistently you build an image of yourself and your company as people who are interested in the readers of that group and who care about the people they help. And it also keeps you at the front of people's minds.

Forming your own newsgroup

Another approach is to form your own group, dedicated to people with a problem with ... (whatever). The big computer companies have snagged onto this one, and there are now many groups covering their products. You could do the same.

Summary

To use groups to build your brand and develop a relationship with your customers and potential customers:

(a) Be constantly and consistently helpful.

(b) Avoid any blatant advertising.

(c) Respond quickly to any public grumbles about your company.

(d) Be seen to come quickly to someone's aid.

Using newsgroups as a public relations vehicle

I've lost count of the number of press releases I've seen posted into groups. They don't work, and they're often resented. But you can still tell everyone about your wonderful new gadget without annoying people in the group.

Again, look for messages where people need help with something. If someone posts in and gripes about the appalling customer service at such-and-such company, you could post in, suggest a way to complain to them effectively, point out that you've just won an award for customer service, ask them to drop you a line and offer a discount off your products.

One superb piece of PR in a newsgroup concerned a lady in dire straits. Her beloved dog needed an expensive operation, which meant she would be forced to sell her car. A veterinary supply company, which manufactured products for dogs, posted a message in the newsgroup saying they would pay for the operation and keep people in touch with the dog's progress on their web site. The operation cost 1,000, but hits to their site increased by 150 per cent, and the company's name became very well known and well regarded amongst the various dog groups all over the internet. The project also secured the company some valuable PR in national newspapers, magazines, big web sites and other media. Now that's clever PR. And their sales showed a worthwhile increase.

Questions and answers

There are so many groups in so many places, how can I keep track of what's happening in all of them?

The simple answer is you can't. You need to choose carefully which groups you think will best serve your company and cultivate those. This takes time to do, but when you've found your key groups, you can use them for a long time.

You seem to advocate a 'touchy-feely' way of using groups for marketing. Isn't that a bit over the top?

Let's answer that question with another question. When was the last time your bank manager sent you a get-well card when you were ill? Marketing is seen by consumers, clients and customers to be an impersonal, mass-market, everyone-is-a-number activity. The internet is unique in that it lets you get on a more personal level with your potential clients and customers, as well as your other customers. It is so rarely seen that it stands out and is commented on. That can't be bad for your company, can it?

Using direct email without any nasty side-effects

Let's clear up one myth straight off. Buying a list of email prospects and then emailing them with your promotional material is not going to (a) make you huge profits, (b) make you the internet's next best friend, or (c) do much for your company image online. Tempted by the thought of lower costs than using conventional direct mail, many companies try this, and then find themselves in a huge credibility mess. Many don't survive the experience.

Yes, you can use direct email as part of your internet marketing. You just have to do it in a different way. You need to use your own mailing list (gathered from your web site) of people who are interested in receiving mail from you.

Using an email list as a selling tool......................................

The European Union has been hard at work developing so-called 'anti-**spam**' directives, so it's worth reading up on them before you plan your direct email campaign. Basically you must allow people a way of getting off your list quickly and easily and do so, you must allow them to 'opt-in' not put them on it yourself. Also check UK legislation and the Data Protection Act, as these are also being updated.

Here are a few tips for using direct email:

1. Always offer people the option to come off your mailing list, and when they ask to be taken off, take them off.
2. Only write to people when you have something to say to them
3. Keep the number of messages down .. once a month (twice at a push) is best.
4. Offer your customers and potential customers something for staying on the list.
5. If possible 'individualise' the messages. That is, put something in them that appeals to that particular person.
6. Keep the message as short as possible.
7. Use a strong headline in the subject line.
8. Respond quickly to messages that come in.

There are now available lists of people who have said they are willing to read commercial emails sent to them. The jury is still very much out on whether or not these lists work. Some recipients are paid so much for each message they read, and many don't read them anyway. It is far better to use your own list, rather than buy one from a third party.

Fig. 36. Advertising an aromatherapy product in a newsgroup about aromatherapy.

If you work your list consistently, and with the right message, they can be successful. If you take the time to listen to what people tell you in their replies, respond promptly, and make them good offers and other 'freebies', your list could well be a goldmine for your company.

Subject: Essential Oils Wholesale
Date: Tue, 30 Mar 1999 23:49:22 -0800
From: <fragrances@jps.net>
Newsgroups: alt.aromatherapy

Visit our site for wholesale information on essential oils of Lavender, orange, lemon grass, Eucalyptus, and many more.
http://www.essentialessences.com

You will need to manage your list, just as you manage your offline list, to keep it fresh and productive. A special newsletter sent to people on your list is often appreciated by the people on it. The more special and welcome you make your list feel, the more likely they are to buy. Email by its nature is a personal medium, so make the most of that personal feel. Very few companies do, preferring to send 'regulation' messages. The companies who do take the time to get to know their customers and treat them professionally and courteously are the ones who are making the money.

Question and answer

What if you don't have an email list of prospects and clients? How can I use direct email?

Make getting a list your priority. Many of your customers probably already have an email address, so try them first. Then, when you have your site up and running, use that to get more people onto your list. You don't need a list with a million people on it. You want a list full of people who are interested in your company and in buying from you. Quality, not quantity, is what counts here. But be aware of legislation that covers Internet mailing lists!

Using online seminars to market your business

One of the best places for online seminars is the online provider Compu-Serve. Here you can find a seminar on just about every subject. Each one is popular with CompuServe's customers. Seminars allow you to do several things at once:

(a) build your company brand

(b) build customer relations

(c) position your company as an expert

(d) make valuable new contacts

(e) build sales leads.

Seminars can be on any subject. The most popular are ones where there is a main theme, with a question and answer session afterwards.

How to hold a seminar

There are several ways you can hold a seminar:

(a) Have one on your web site.

(b) Hold one on a ready-made service such as CompuServe.

(c) Take part in an existing seminar.

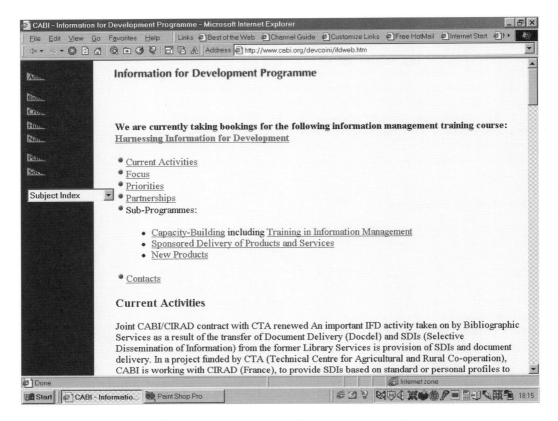

Fig. 37. CABI is an example of an organisation which runs online seminars (in this case, on the topic of information management).

The pros and cons of running a seminar on your own web site

The pros

▷ You can direct people through your web site.

▷ You can use the mailing list generated yourself, without having to buy it.

▷ You have total control over what is said and done.

Fig. 38. CLE Online is another company which offers online seminars. If you register, it offers to keep you informed of all new seminars.

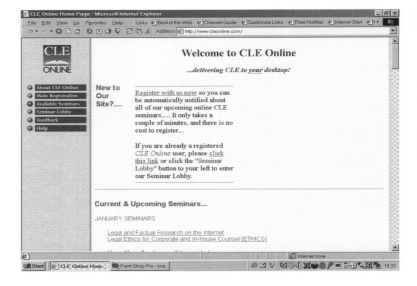

The cons

▷ The time it takes to set up, organise and promote the seminar.

▷ The number of people needed to help out.

▷ People may have difficulties getting on the site to listen in.

The pros and cons of running a seminar on a ready-made service

The pros

▷ They do a lot of the hard work for you.

▷ They'll moderate the discussion.

▷ They'll promote the seminar for you.

▷ No problems with people trying to visit the seminar.

The cons

▷ You may have to buy the generated mailing list.

▷ You don't have as much control.

Promoting your seminars

Seminars can be excellent business builders if they're managed correctly. They are certainly worth trying, at least once. One advantage of holding them online is that you don't have to stand up in front of lots of people to speak.

Seminars can be promoted in places such as usenet, your web site, offline magazines, online magazines and by using your mailing list. If you intend using seminars it is important to keep a transcript of the seminar which can be downloaded from your site – many people miss out on seminars they would like to visit (because of time constraints), and in this way they and you get the benefit even if they're not there for the real thing.

Question and answer

I'm nervous about holding a seminar. Is there anywhere I can get more detailed information about running one online?

Not that we know of. The best way to see if they are for you is to take part in a few yourself, or even get involved with the running of one. This way you'll find out more about what's involved. You could also contact the speakers at a seminar and ask them for advice.

Finally...

The number of ways you can market your business online is enormous and, as the internet develops, more and more ways will appear. The key to success is being prepared to devote sufficient time and effort to what you do – and aim for quality responses rather than thousands of maybes.

Case Studies

George makes more of his marketing

George has marketed his business using usenet for a year, and he's happy with the results he's getting. But George has had no success with using forums and special interest groups. Someone has almost always had a go at him. Also, his carefully thought out messages just bring barrowloads of nasty mail.

One helpful moderator suggests that George's style is okay for usenet, but that people in other groups find it rather wearing, and feel talked down to. George spends the next month carefully reading the groups he's failed in, and soon spots a pattern in the way people communicate there. Unfortunately, his writing manner stays the same and, despite making some changes to his messaging style, he still gets loads of hostile mail.

Christine spots her problem

Christine has recently bought an email list from a company that sells lists of people interested in receiving promotional material. She mails the entire 2,000 people on her list, and only gets one enquiry. She decides it must have been a bad time to mail and tries again in a month's time. The result is just the same.

On a business mailing list Christine hears other people's tales of woe about using bought mailing lists. Many of their experiences were even worse than hers. Some people have bought them from people who **spam** the internet.

During this time registrations on her site have been slowly increasing, and Christine decides that though her list is smaller, maybe she should give it a try. She gets a much better response, and plenty of ideas for other marketing projects are generated from her list. Small can be beautiful.

Fig. 39. Internet mailing lists can be a very good method of marketing your business online. How about developing your own mailing list, to keep your own customers informed of what you do? 'The Mailing List.net' web site can help you do this.

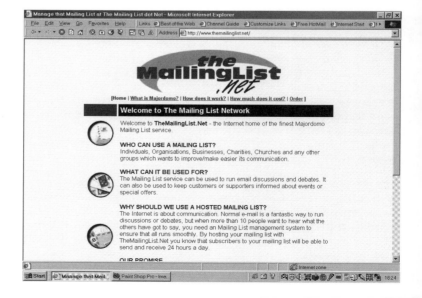

8 Building your online brand

In this chapter we will explore:

▶ *why online branding will be vital to your success*

▶ *the right way to build your brand image*

▶ *getting your brand known online*

▶ *what you can learn from brands already online.*

. . . .

Why online branding is vital to your success

Brands are as important to business success online as they are offline. However, mass market brands do not always transfer well into the online world. This is great news for many smaller companies, which do not have the massive budgets needed to build a successful brand in the real world. Many people remember web sites primarily by their brand image. This is why it is so important that everything you do on your site, and in your online marketing, harmonises and works together with the brand image you want to portray.

Elements of a brand image
Your brand image will comprise a number of elements including:

1. your choice of domain name

2. your design and use of an artworked logo

3. the use of key slogan phrases or straplines

4. the colour scheme used on your site

5. the use of type fonts on your site

6. the style in which you answer emails.

All of these elements should be consistent with and support the brand image you wish to project. A well-developed brand is probably the single most powerful weapon in marketing in the world today. Consider Coca Cola, McDonald's, Wrigleys, Virgin, Microsoft, Toys' Я 'Us, to name just a few strongly branded companies. A strong brand can cross almost any geographic, linguistic, economic or social boundary in the modern world. Yet very few companies appear to develop a proper branding strategy. Possibly this is because it seems such a difficult policy to carry through consistently, let alone do well – although it is not really as difficult as it sounds once you get the basic systems in place to deliver it.

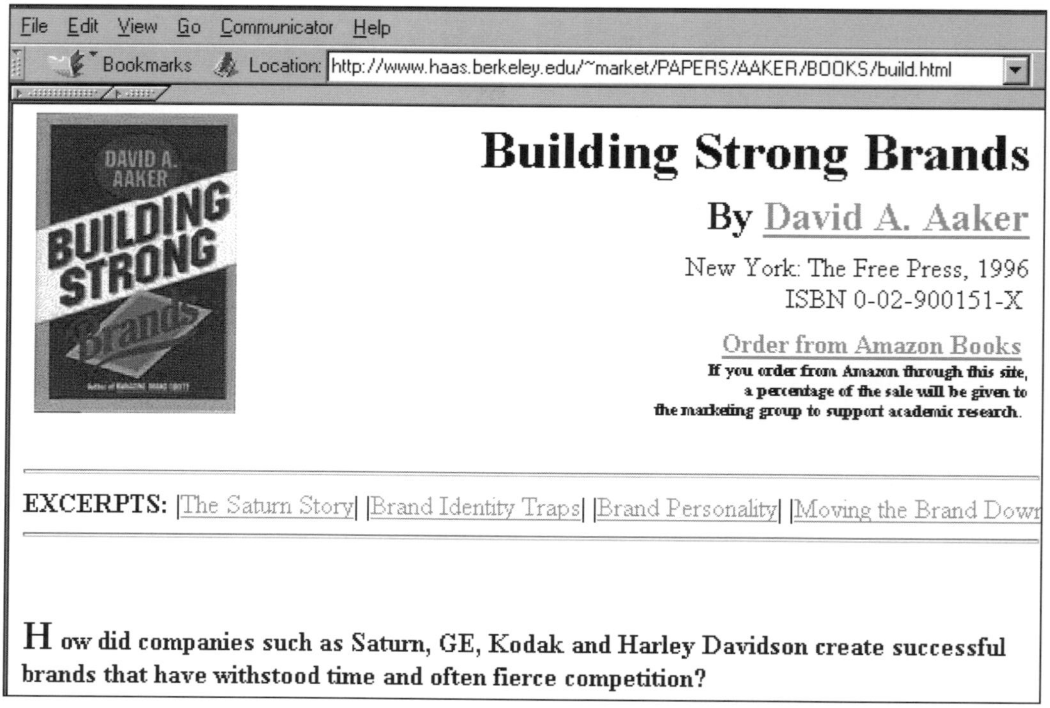
File Edit View Go Communicator Help
Bookmarks Location: http://www.haas.berkeley.edu/~market/PAPERS/AAKER/BOOKS/build.html
DAVID A. AAKER
BUILDING STRONG Brands
Building Strong Brands
By David A. Aaker
New York: The Free Press, 1996
ISBN 0-02-900151-X
Order from Amazon Books
If you order from Amazon through this site, a percentage of the sale will be given to the marketing group to support academic research.
EXCERPTS: |The Saturn Story| |Brand Identity Traps| |Brand Personality| |Moving the Brand Dow
How did companies such as Saturn, GE, Kodak and Harley Davidson create successful brands that have withstood time and often fierce competition?

Fig. 40. *Building Strong Brands* – one of many examples of brand development resources you can discover through the internet.

Mention certain web sites or company names, such as Yahoo!, Web Pages That Suck, or Amazon, and many people will immediately be able to tell you something about that company or web site, and what it does. This is the goal you need to achieve if you are to dominate *your* niche. If people do not recognise you, then you will have an uphill job making a success of your online marketing. Yet building a brand is simply a matter of understanding its importance, and then taking the time and trouble needed to organise and implement it.

A brand strategy

1. Your online brand is the one marketing tool you must get right.
2. You do not need to spend massive sums to develop an effective online brand. Time and effort count for more.
3. Your company only needs to become well known to its target market – not to the world at large.
4. Everything you say and do online must be consistent with your brand image.
5. Building a brand requires time, effort and planning.

Question and answer

Our company is only a small business. Surely going to all the time and effort of developing an online brand isn't worth it for us?

It doesn't matter whether you are a massive multinational or a small shop in the back end of nowhere. Your online brand will be by far your most powerful tool for internet marketing. People recognise brands, and brand behaviour. And if those brands and behaviour are consistent, people will respond favourably to them, in the case of a business by buying its products or services.

Building your brand image

Everything that has come before in this book will help build your brand image. But you have to know what sort of image this should be, before you can put it into action. Maybe you already have an established brand and image that you use in the real world. You can take or adapt that and put it online. If your brand image is a bit muddled or non-existent, here are some pointers to help you clarify and develop it online:

(a) Decide what is the single most important thing your company stands for.

(b) Decide on a basic colour scheme that represents what your company stands for and its market profile. For example, should the colour scheme be bold and bright, or sober and understated?

(c) Draw up a 'charter' for each aspect of your business such as responding to emails, dealing with complaints, delivering products or services, and answering the phone; then put this charter into operation. It won't do any good by hanging on a wall in the office.

(d) In creating or developing the brand, make sure you involve every individual member of staff who will be dealing with customers online.

(e) Develop systems for every function you carry out online. Check the resources section of this book for information on doing this.

(f) Be genuinely interested in your customers – their needs, wants, grumbles, everything.

These should be the cornerstones of your online brand. Let's look at it from a business point of view. A brand is not just some kind of marketing aid; a brand should embody your company's whole attitude towards everyone it deals with, from suppliers to customers, staff and the media. It is a tragedy to see so many companies spending thousands of pounds designing online brands, which are simply not backed up by their actions. That brand can quickly fall into disrepute, and be associated in everyone's minds with bad service. Once established, that negative attitude can be very hard to shift, and will almost certainly require the development of a completely new brand from scratch. Remember the case of Ratners, the high street jewellery brand?

Laying the right foundations

So what steps can you take to lay the foundations of your brand image online? Any of the following would be a good start. All of them can help you build a strong brand.

1. Use banner ads and similar devices to promote awareness of your company.

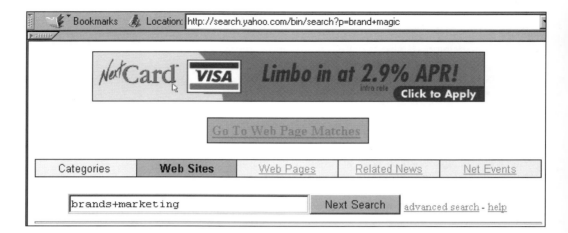

Fig. 41. An example of a banner ad (promoting an internet credit card).

2. Sponsor relevant events, sites, competitions, conferences or other happenings.

3. Be seen to be active in newsgroups and forums – not with sales 'puffery' but by offering genuine worthwhile information and help.

4. Use 'flash-points' about your company in newsgroups to your advantage, supported by some intelligent public relations.

5. Never let any criticism of your company go unanswered online. By taking the right action at the right time, you can quickly forestall any 'company bashing' that might develop and damage your reputation.

6. Always deliver more than you promise.

7. Be the first to offer something in your field, a new product or service of some kind.

8. Use a catchy – but not tacky – word to sum up your brand image.

9. Be the first in your market segment to offer something new and different on your web site.

10. Use every opportunity you can for off- and online public relations.

11. Remember that every transaction, every event, and every visitor who comes to your site present new opportunities to develop your brand online. Find a word or phrase, or simple image, that sums up your company and everything about it, and then get it known to the people who need to know about it.

12. Building a major brand like Yahoo! requires a substantial budget, but remember that unlike Yahoo! you should not be trying to target all 30 million people online. Your aim should be to capture the percentage of those who either use or could use your product or service, in your chosen niche. This is a vital distinction. Ignore the masses: go for the people who you know will buy, and leave the mega-branding to those with the money to chase the world.

13. Get yourself associated with everything you can that has to do with your market and your market's interests. This could involve forms of participation such as:

> newsgroups
> forums
> seminars
> charity work
> sponsorship
> helping to fund a project
> supporting your trade magazine

There are many, many possibilities, and it's up to you to exploit them.

Question and answer

It sounds as if building your brand is only one part of the process, the other being maintaining it. Isn't that unfeasible for companies who are somewhat smaller than, say, Amazon.com?

This is true. Building the brand is one thing, but then you have to maintain it. Amazon, whom we will discuss shortly, is a prime example of a company which has built and maintained its online brand superbly well. But do keep in mind that you don't need to brand-build on the scale of Amazon. Your name simply needs to be known to the people who will potentially buy your products or services and to your existing customers. The rest of the online population is irrelevant. Above all, your brand must dominate your own particular niche.

More tips and techniques for building a brand online

Here is a checklist of ways you can develop your brand online:

1. Buy banner advertising on sites that your prospects use.
2. Sponsor a specific section of someone else's web site.
3. Sponsor a specific section of one or more newsletters or e-zines.
4. Arrange for your company's technical experts to be available to contribute to newsgroups and online newsletters.
5. Develop an effective PR campaign.
6. Offer something new and exciting for free download or access.
7. Win high customer approval by adopting and promoting a cause in your industry, such as health and safety, or youth training.
8. Get your company or site talked about.
9. Be seen to be innovative – in your products, services and approach to problem-solving and to customer relations.
10. Encourage customers to talk about their successes with your products or services.

Aim to make yourself highly visible in your chosen niche. It almost has to be the case that people cannot move within that niche without running across your name. And this doesn't have to be expensive. Many facilities and services on the internet are free (for example, newsgroups), or reasonably cheap, so you don't need to spend pots of money. Just be willing to take the time to grasp every opportunity that presents itself, and if none does, then generate some.

Examples of online success stories . . . .

Your best brand-builders are your customers, so ignore them at your peril. Treat them well, and encourage them to talk about you and your products.

Question and answer

What's wrong with targeting the wider world with our message?

A great deal. It will create confusion in the minds of people who are not buying and using your products and who have no need to. It will confuse prospective customers in your target market, because they will not feel completely sure what your company stands for. Targeting the wider world costs a great deal of money, and since budgets are limited such expenditure would inevitably reduce and dilute the impact of what you're doing. You only need the right people to hear about you. Don't let yourself be drowned out in the noise of thousands of other brands talking at once.

Learning from successful online brands

From a marketing point of view, the most interesting brands are the ones that began life online. Amazon.com is one of these. The Amazon brand is so completely identified with online bookselling that it would be almost impossible for the company to move out of that sphere and succeed in a different one. It would seem very strange, and confusing, if Amazon suddenly began to sell fashion clothing or airline tickets.

▷ Amazon has built its brand with superb products, amazing customer service, an easy-to-use and informative site, help from their customers in the form of book reviews, and personalities such as Oprah Winfrey adding newsworthy interest to their site. They have developed an 'associate program' for sites wanting to sell Amazon's products, and treat everyone they deal with in a systematic but friendly manner. You can learn a huge amount from the way Amazon continues to develop its brand, capturing a bigger share of the global bookselling market with every month that passes. Amazon is a classic case study of how an online enterprise got the business basics right first, and then built the brand. Your brand will not survive very long if you do not get the business foundations right at the outset.

▷ Java, the programming language developed by Sun Microsystems, is another example of superb branding. Java is a quirky and distinctive but easy-to-remember name, in any language. Java makes many people think of coffee. That idea has been used to get Java endless online and offline coverage. Books, web sites and many other projects and products have been spun off this single brand. Millions of internet users everywhere are now aware of Java – even if many of them are still not quite sure what it is!

▷ Both Java and Amazon are now massive companies, but what about smaller ones? One Yorkshire bakery (Mailacake) effectively built up its brand by being the first to deliver cakes and other goods when they had been ordered online. They followed the 'be first' rule and

Fig. 42. Lillian Too's Little Book of Feng Shui. This site is a good example of making the most of a trend – in this case, Feng Shui.

did very well with it. Their site became very well known, and people started thinking of them as 'the' internet bakery. If you want Yorkshire bakery items, then you have only one place to go, despite the best efforts of their rivals to seize their brand dominance from them.

▷ Lillian Too, the renowned expert, has also built her brand effectively online. Whenever the subject of Feng Shui comes up on the internet, her name is mentioned, and people flock to her site to find out more. Before she began using the internet, Lillian Too had already built up a loyal following with her books about Feng Shui, and she is now using the internet to capitalise still further on that success.

▷ The UK internet service provider Demon Internet has grown from a tiny company into a large business, thanks to its careful brand building. Demon rarely advertised the company, but in the early days of the internet in the UK it built up a brand image of the service provider at a 'tenner a month'. That concept served them well and, despite some problems of a technical nature, their brand image has been strong enough to see off any negative publicity in that regard. The

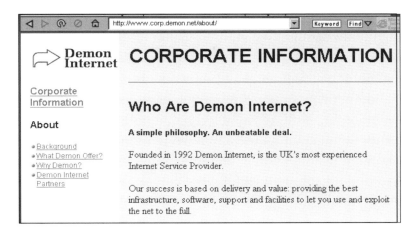

Fig. 43. Clive Stanford made millions from developing Demon Internet as a strongly branded internet service provider which attracted a very loyal following.

original Demon entrepreneur, Clive Stanford, was subsequently able to sell this very successfully branded business to ScottishTelecom for many millions of pounds.

Businesses in the UK have been painfully slow to take advantage of online brand-building. Forward-looking companies like Demon Internet have planned ahead, and made the most of every opportunity, often creating many new opportunities of their own. In just a few years they have reaped enormous rewards. Your company can do the same. By following the advice in this chapter you can start building your online brand. It is not too late. The internet is still only just beginning, but all around the world entrepreneurs are learning fast, and the competition is intensifying, driven by the prospect of vast rewards. Your next step is to develop a strategic plan to help you beat your competitors, and discover how to make the most of internet trends, which we will cover in the next chapter.

Question and answer

What are the key things that these companies have done to make their online branding so successful?

The key ingredients are these:

1. They have planned ahead.

2. They have taken the time to understand how the internet works and how it differs from the real world.

3. They look after their customers personally as never before.

4. They use systems as much as possible to ensure consistent quality of performance.

5. They produce quality products or services.

6. Their customer service is exemplary.

7. They have learned from their mistakes, and listened to their customers.

8. They are consistently good at what they do.

CASE STUDIES

Bill gets branded
Bill's company is targeting a small and specialist niche, and his colleagues do not really think he can be so ambitious as to build a brand for his company. Bill spends a week or so reading newsgroups and checking web sites, and is rather surprised to find that there could be quite a few more possibilities than he thought. He sets aside a budget and buys banner ads, and sends material to the most relevant sites. A friend tells him about a thread on a newsgroup where Bill could post. He helps out

the person concerned and his web site hits rise dramatically. As a result he sells more of his product online in a single week than he has in the entire six months before! Many people comment favourably about Bill's friendly and helpful style online.

Maggie misses the boat
Maggie has also been using banner ads and other ways of building her company image. A few months ago she had problems with her delivery system, but has now sorted this out. While checking a newsgroup she notices a thread about her subject, in which one writer complains about the terrible delivery problems he had with her company. Maggie decides to let that one go. Since the group is small she doesn't think anyone will notice the message. Her competitor jumps in and offers the writer a product for free as a goodwill gesture. Maggie realises that she has made a big mistake and emails the writer personally offering two of her products for free. But he's not interested and takes his business 'to a company which really does care about its customers.' Maggie retires, hurt, to a quiet corner to think again about the implications of marketing online.

9 Making a long-term success of your online marketing

In this chapter we will explore:

▶ *how to beat your competitors online*

▶ *powerful internet trends you can profit from*

▶ *the five keys to future online marketing success.*

. . . .

How to beat your competitors online

It's easy to be 'blown away' by the success of your online marketing efforts and therefore forget to keep marketing. Like so many things in life, online marketing requires constant attention, though not to the high degree that is necessary when you first start out. No doubt the success of your site and your efforts will soon be spotted by your competitors, and they will try to 'steal' some of your hard work. This is where a **marketing plan** becomes a valuable ally. It can help you beat the competition and keep your site on the road to continued success.

Your marketing plan should include the following:

1. Your key marketing areas such as usenet, seminars and so on.

2. Who, on your staff, will be responsible for doing what.

3. Contingency plans in case of problems.

4. How often you'll publish your e-zine, update your web site and with what features or content.

5. Data collection from your mailing list and online forum.

6. When you will do checks on competitors' sites, new sites, newly formed newsgroups and so on.

7. When you will have meetings to discuss strategy and tactics.

8. The systems you will use to analyse your site and marketing efforts.

9. Your goals for your online marketing, the results you want and how you'll get them.

Many companies market their sites heavily for several months and then gradually give up, only to start marketing positively again when they see a rival competitor grabbing their market share. Your marketing plan will give you an edge over your competitors. It will allow you to focus on the results you want, without the distraction of having to play leap frog with your competitors.

Tips and techniques

So how else can you beat the competition? Here are some key tips and techniques:

(a) **Be unique.** The uniqueness need not necessarily be in your company, but in your web site, the unique way you talk to your online visitors, the unique way you sell to them.

(b) **Be interactive.** This doesn't mean loading your pages with flashy graphics, animations and scrolling banners. What kind of interactive content could actually be found useful by your customers?

(c) **Find out what your customers want** and then give it to them! This sounds simple and obvious, but it is rarely done well.

(d) **Develop a core group of customers** who are willing to let you try out new marketing approaches on them. Debug and generally check your site fully before you launch new marketing approaches.

(e) **Make your web site a 'living site'** – one that grows and evolves with the internet and in response to your customers.

(f) **Care about your customers.** Again this is something often said, but rarely done well.

(g) **Respond to customers' complaints and comments,** and treat them with the same respect and professionalism you would want yourself.

(h) **Appoint a 'key' person** to answer email, someone with whom customers can build a confident relationship.

All these elements can be structured into your marketing plan, and into your existing business plan, with little difficulty. Try and direct more of your efforts towards your existing customers, encouraging them to visit the site, as well as attracting new customers. Existing customers feel more valued when they have special sections dedicated to them. The 'ongoing' feeling that a web site creates will help you do more business with them.

Question and answer

Is a marketing plan really necessary or worthwhile for a business such as mine, with just a small web site?

Yes! No matter how small your site, having and maintaining a marketing plan for it will help keep you focused on what you want it to achieve, and will help bring in a continuing stream of visitors and sales leads.

Powerful internet trends you can profit from

None of us has access to a crystal ball, and assessing future trends is an ongoing problem for internet marketers, as with all business people. But here are some important trends which are already clearly emerging, together with some predictions about what could happen, and how you can profit from them.

E-business

E-business, as I predicted in the previous edition of this book, has taken off. Despite the stockmarket hammerings of the big names, e-business is still alive and well. What we have seen and are seeing is simply a clear-out of those businesses that would never have worked anyway.

The message is loud and clear, Old Economy rules, with a New Economy twist. Putting dot com after your company name is no longer enough. Those who compete on price are going to be hardest hit in the future. But quality will win out in the end.

To profit from this key trend, you will need to have the business systems in place to deal properly with the enquiries your web site generates, and to put into action some of the details discussed above. And look after your customers as you've never looked after them before. Neglect them, and pay the price.

The growing trend of one-to-one marketing

I wrote in the first edition of this book that this would be a growing trend. And it has been to a degree. New laws covering e-mail have cut it back somewhat, and now I would say that personalisation in itself is no longer enough. In fact, it's getting a bit over done.

What is still missing is people.

Without a real person behind a computer it doesn't work. The skill is to combine the best of what we can do as people with the best of what computers and software can do.

For large corporations, this is going to be an expensive struggle, but for smaller independent companies it offers a vital competitive edge. So to profit from it, combine the computers, the data and your people to deliver a really personalised service to your customers. Before the sale, during the sale, and after the sale.

The global electronic village

It nearly happened. Instead, internet globalisation, a subtly different beast, beat the global electronic village to it. The knack here is not to fall into the indifference trap. Just because you and I speak English, it doesn't mean everyone else does or wants to. Sites need to allow people to access your site in their language. They need to reflect local selling techniques, local customs, for example.

Classical Music Web Ring

The Classical Music Web Ring is a chain of many hundreds of classical music web sites.

You can jump from site to site, choose a random site or view a list of all the member sites.

Give the Classical Music Web Ring a test drive using this sample:

"Site title here" is part of
The Classical Music Web Ring
The free linking service sponsored by Classical Music UK
Show me: [Previous] [Random] [Next] [Next 5] [All]

Fig. 44. An example of a web ring, in this case a ring of sites devoted to classical music.

But all the time have that global feel.
Even if your main market is the UK, you can easily find you have customers coming from countries you never anticipated. Don't ignore them, embrace them!

Globalisation has also meant new opportunities for partnering with other companies here and abroad. Something which few companies seem that willing to do. Preferring to give lip service to the idea. But if you can embrace it, it will help your site and business grow.

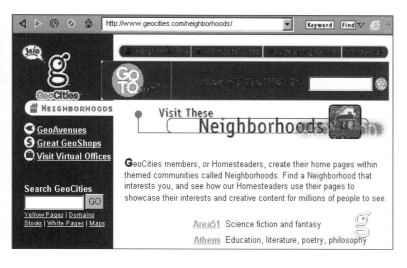

Fig. 45. Geocities, an outstanding example of a virtual community, with more than three million members. The community is divided into special interest 'neighborhoods'.

The keys to successful online marketing ....

Question and answer

How do I know that these trends are happening now?

These trends are based on many years of watching, marketing, talking, listening and data-crunching. Few companies get in on the crest of a trend wave, but those that do can do very well indeed. Indeed, by taking the time to watch how the internet develops, you can help predict the trends yourself.

The five keys to online marketing success

It takes a combination of elements to make a success of internet marketing, but there are five key steps you can take to make a success of yours:

1. *Get your web site right*

Get your web site right before you start marketing. Make sure the content is right, and the navigation is right. Be sure that it is specifically designed to build your brand, and really gets across your business focus. Your web site is your 'face' on the internet. If there are spelling mistakes, forms that don't work, different styles on different pages, broken links, odd layouts and so on, it all detracts from the message you're trying to get across. Don't be too ambitious at first. Start small and grow from there.

2. *Know what you want to achieve*

Write down what you want your site and your marketing to do. Do you want to sell products or services direct from your site using secure transaction facilities? Or do you want to use your online marketing to generate qualified leads? Do you eventually want to sell advertising space on your web site? Or do you want your site to sell your products and services only? What about alliances with companies selling to the same customer as you? Do you want to build them or not? Once you have a clear plan of what you want to achieve with your site, you will be one massive step closer to achieving it – and several steps ahead of the competition.

3. *Watch the competition*

No matter how well you niche your company online, there will always be some overlap with what other companies are doing. Spend time finding out what they do online, and try to find out how successful they are. Learn from both their successes and their mistakes. And remember, they are likely to be watching you, too.

4. *Stay with it*

Be consistent, persistent and forward-looking. Lack of consistency ruins marketing, more than many other things. Everything you say, do and operate must be consistent with your company goals. This will help you enormously in building a broad brand image in people's minds about who you are, what you stand for and, most importantly, what you sell. Persistence is another key to success. If you give up at the first obstacle or bad week, you'll never make it. So tough it out. Learn from your mistakes and build on others' success strategies. And most important of all, be forward-looking. Watch for trends, read up on the latest techniques and strategies, innovate, and be everything your customers want you to be.

5. *Be innovative, unique and customer-focused*
Being the same as everyone else on the web is easy, but if you want to be successful, then you need to be innovative, unique and constantly focused on your customers and clients, as well as your visitors. Innovation does not need to be something totally brand new. For example, it could be a 'return on investment calculator' that visitors can use on your web site. It could consist of any feature that is slighly different, but which also has a practical value to your visitors.

Question and answer

This all sounds too simplistic. Do these keys really work?

Yes, based on extensive experience, they certainly do! They are just some of the keys used by some of the internet's most successful companies and operations. They are tried and tested, and when they are used consistently and carefully they work. Try them and discover the benefits for yourself.

Case studies

Suzanne's successful site
Suzanne has built an excellent site, and one that her existing customers come back to often. She has worked hard on ways of keeping potential clients visiting. So far they are coming back in droves, often recommending her site to friends and colleagues. But she realises this is just the start of her internet marketing. She takes a week away from her site, to develop a marketing plan in conjunction with her staff. Suzanne feels that their input will help the site develop as they bring in new ideas of their own. It will also give those staff members a valuable new skill, which will be to the benefit of her business. Suzanne and her staff together build a 'living marketing plan' and then go out and 'live it' with great success.

Derek's 'dead in the water' site
Derek's site has been successful, too. He has found an excellent, little-exploited niche, and carefully constructed both his web site and his company around it. He has been on holiday for two weeks, and returns to find that hundreds of enquiries have come in since he went away. One

of Derek's staff is keen to get involved with the web site, too, but Derek believes it is too much hassle training the employee. Besides, the web site is his 'baby'. He leaves the site as it is and carries on with other pressing work, confidently expecting the level of enquiries to continue. Indeed, they do for several weeks, until they dry up almost overnight. Derek has been banking on those enquiries coming in, and has cut back his traditional marketing. He ends up having a frantic two months trying to market both his site and his business to generate new work. Derek takes to heart a comment from someone who visited his site, saying that he had visited the site four times and had not seen anything new on it for weeks.

10 Marketing mailing lists online

In this chapter we will explore:

▶ *online marketing mailing lists, what they are and how to use them*
▶ *a selection of online marketing lists you can subscribe to.*

. . . .

Online marketing mailing lists

What they are and how to use them
Since the earliest days of the internet, people have been joining 'mailing lists' to talk about their favourite topics via email. Mailing lists are a valuable aspect of the internet. They are a very handy way of receiving regular information on a vast range of different topics. Once you have subscribed, the latest news and information items from the mailing list will be downloaded into your email daily, weekly or at other intervals. To subscribe to a mailing list, all you usually have to do is send an email request to the list operator. Sometimes you are asked to include some keywords in your application, such as 'subscribe', to help the list operators manage what may be a large amount of incoming mail.

Most mailing lists are completely free. They are usually owned and maintained by individuals who keep them going as a labour of love, as a service to fellow professionals and enthusiasts, or as a promotional add-on to a particular net-based service. This chapter contains a selection of mailing lists intended for business managers and marketing professionals. If you would like to search for possible mailing lists yourself, probably the best place to start – and probabaly the most popular one – is:

List-Link International
http://www.list-link.com
The List-Link database offers access to up-to-date and detailed information about mailing lists and their suppliers. You can register for free and get a 15-day free trial of a comprehensive database of mailing lists and their sources, and discover lists of all sectors world wide and who owns them. There are regular updates, news/press releases and offers. The List-Link database is researched by offices located in the United Kingdom and France. The database is uploaded regularly to the web. As well as having access to the largest mailing list resource database, taking out a subscription gives you discounted rates on news services and on-site advertising. You'll get up to 25 per cent off the price of banner advertising and content placement.

Liszt
http://www.liszt.com
Liszt is probably the best known and most used database source of

Fig. 46. Liszt is a web site well worth exploring by the business user. It contains a searchable database of literally thousands of internet mailing lists, covering every subject under the sun.

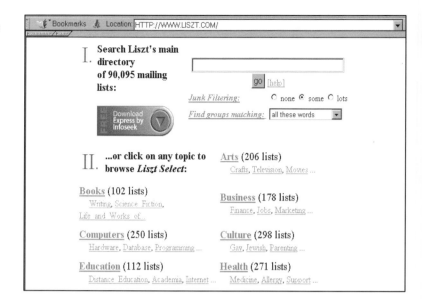

mailing lists on the internet. Its main directory contains more than 90,000 mailing lists, and hundreds of new ones are added each week.

Mailbase
http://www.mailbase.ac.uk/
Mailbase provides electronic discussion lists for the UK higher education community. It has over 2,000 discussion lists and 160,000 members world wide.

ONElist
http://www.onelist.com/subscribe.cgi/marketplace
ONElist is a mailing list system that allows its members to create and manage email lists or subscribe to a wide variety of existing lists. It's quick and easy, and it's free. In minutes, you can be part of your own email community.

Fig. 47. If you want to market to the UK educational community, Mailbase is a must for you. It contains more than 2,000 different mailing lists, with more than 160,000 subscribers, interested in everything from teaching English to school trips and education management.

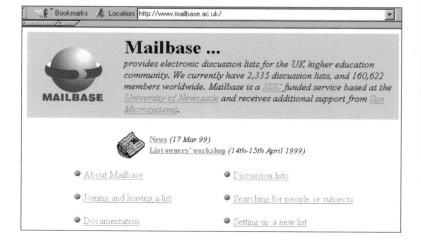

Fig. 48. Visit the ONElist web site if you would like to learn more about creating and managing your own internet mailing lists.

Fig. 49. Sparklist is another useful resource where you can find out about internet-based mailing lists.

Sparklist
http://www.sparklist.com/
Sparklist offers an easy to use web-based email list-hosting service.

A selection of marketing lists you can subscribe to

Absolute Internet Marketing Resources Ezine
http://www.appalachianmarketing.com
This is a free e-zine that contains various current online marketing resources. To subscribe, send email. Appalachian Online Marketing specialises in online marketing techniques and resources for small, medium and home-based businesses.

Adforum
listserv@unc.edu
This list contains discussions about advertising education. The list owner is Tom Bowers. To find out more, send email to the address above.

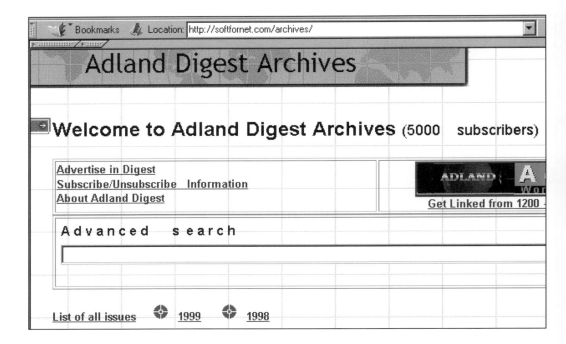

Bookmarks   Location: http://softfornet.com/archives/

Adland Digest Archives

Welcome to Adland Digest Archives (5000 subscribers)

Advertise in Digest
Subscribe/Unsubscribe   Information
About Adland Digest

ADLAND

Get Linked from 1200

Advanced search

List of all issues   1999   1998

Fig. 50. Adland is a marketing mailing list with some 5,000 subscribers. You can search through current and back issues to 1998.

Adland
http://softfornet.com/adland/list.asp
Adland is an email discussion in digest format related to marketing online for those with a small or no budget, and looking for alternative solutions for their online business presence. This mailing list is moderated and distributed in the form of a digest. You are invited to participate, to contribute by helping and also by posting your problems, opinions, questions, concerns. For more information, or to join the list, visit the web site above.

AdverTalk
dms_AdverTalk@fiestanet.com
AdverTalk is an email discussion group for small businesses to discuss issues and offer solutions related to small business marketing, including advertising, public relations, database marketing and sales channels. The moderator is Data Dobson. To find out more, send email to the address above.

AFMNet
http://www.univ-pau.fr/~benavent/inscript.htm
AFMNet was created by the French Marketing Association. Messages can be posted in French or in English in this mailing list. For more information, or to join the list, visit the web site above.

Asian Internet Marketing
http://www.aim.apic.net/
AIM runs an open moderated mailing list for Asian internet marketing and sales pioneers. Subjects of interest to list subscribers include news, commentary and views for Asian internet marketers, Asian marketing/sales-related questions and answers, integrating internet-based marketing tactics with traditional media, overcoming cross-border marketing impedi-

ments in Asia with the net, new internet technologies of benefit to Asian marketers, using Asian languages to market to Asians, selling to a multilingual audience over the net, courses on the internet, legal developments affecting net marketers, meetings, conferences and activities, requests for stories and speakers on internet marketing, announcements of new web sites of interest to Asian internet marketers, job announcements, Asian net personalities/visionaries, internet surveys, book reviews and resources for internet marketers.

Association of Consumer Research
listserv@listserv.okstate.edu
ACR-L is a list with the purpose of discussing consumer research. It serves as a forum for researchers, practitioners and graduate students working in the interdisciplinary field of consumer research. There is a home page for ACR-L and also a page for the Association for Consumer Research. To find out more, send email to the address above.

AutoShoppers
autoshoppers@bbs.hannah.com
AutoShoppers, which has its own web page, is a mailing list dedicated to discussing how autoshoppers, bots (robots), agents and other tools will affect the way we do business and how we may have to adapt to them. The list owner is Frank Atkinson. To find out more, send email to the address above with the text 'subscribe' in the subject.

BizSupport
join-bizsupport@marketserv.com
BizSupport is a business opportunities support forum. It is an unmoderated list covering business opportunities and support of sales organisations. It also welcomes network marketers, MLMers, home-based business enthusiasts and traditional marketers/entrepreneurs. Advertising is permitted if kept to a relative minimum. It does not allow posting by non-subscribers. This list is ad hoc. Material for discussion is not provided by the list manager. There is no digest version or archive. You will receive via auto-messaging its listserver rules and guidelines. Contact the owner Jon Hulett with any questions addressed to the email address above.

Direct Marketing Digest
http://www.argo-navis.com/competence
This list is a mailing list set up to discuss database marketing and relationship management. The owner and moderator is Helmar Rudulph. If you are looking for consulting services, specific web sites, demo versions, evaluations and specific database marketing-related software solutions, you may find it here. This is a site in a constant state of flux, but potentially a very powerful resource. For an introduction, send an empty email to: dm-intro@argo-navis.com

Elmar
elmar-request@columbia.edu
Elmar runs a moderated list for the discussion of marketing and marketing research. Its focus is academic. Archives for Elmar are available. Send

subscription requests to the email address above. The moderator is Peter Palij.

Email Promote
http://www.emailpromote.listbot.com
This is a free email club to promote your business, product or sale without spamming. To subscribe, send email to: badkes@sunline.net

E-Marketing
http://www.webbers.com/emark/
This site runs a mailing list which discusses electronic marketing techniques. Moderated by George Matyjewicz, the *E-Marketing Digest* brings its subscribers an interactive forum where beginner and expert marketers trade information, 'war stories', resources, opinions and advice on internet marketing strategies. A recent selection of 'how to' articles on the site included e-mail marketing, newsgroup marketing, using autoresponders, designing a sig file, effective writing skills, and an online marketer's toolkit. The list owner is Gary Foote. You can subscribe by visiting the E-Marketing web site.

E-Tailer's Digest
http://www.gapent.com/etailer/
The E-Tailer's Digest is a resource for retail professionals on the net. It is published in a moderated digest form every Monday, Wednesday and Friday. Its discussion topics include any and all subjects that pertain to retailing. Such subjects typically include: interaction with customers, psychographics, point-of-sale software solutions, point-of-purchase displays, security issues, effective merchandising and open-to-buy, mail order issues, shipping and tax issues, accounting and legal issues, public relations, promotions and advertising, online marketing, differen-

Fig. 51. Marketing Competence, another sales-related mailing list on the internet. It includes editorial features and a discussion forum.

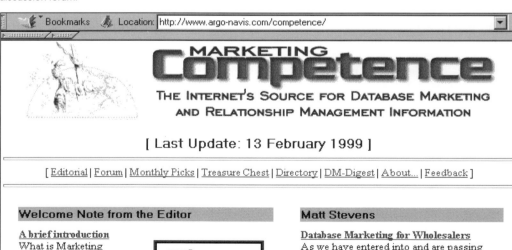

tiation, doing business internationally and effective web-site design. The list owner is George Matyjewicz. To subscribe, visit the web site or send email to etd@gapent.com with a subject of SUBSCRIBE_ETD.

Euro-Business
http://www.cgtd.com/global/euro/euro.htm
Euro-Business has a web page with subscription information and extensive documentation. It offers news briefs, analysis, opinions, questions, reports, forecasts and tips on products, markets, areas, business opportunities, contacts for trade, export, import and investment information. It is a moderated forum for discussing, exchanging, commenting on news, views, issues, opinions on practices, customs and conducting business in modern Europe. Whether you are looking to strengthen your business links or looking to do business there for the first time, or want to know the consumer trends or economic facts or down-to-earth advice on how to conduct yourself or just inform yourself, Euro-Business could be for you. The moderator is Prav Kaps.

EventWeb
http://www.eventweb.com/
EventWeb addresses the interactive marketing needs of meeting, conference and trade show promoters, educators, organisers and webmasters. It runs a mailing list which is also a discussion list, and which includes a monthly digest. The EventWeb newsletter offers internet marketing guidance to meeting, conference and trade show producers. The newsletter offers personalisation options. When you subscribe you can select the types of editorial content and sponsorship information you wish to receive. Simply put a Y for Yes next to the information you wish to receive and an N for No if you do not wish to receive certain types of content. Once you subscribe, it is easy to change your customised settings. If your orga-

nisation uses the web to promote your events, you could benefit from subscribing to EventWeb. You will be joining over 3,200 industry professionals from more than 35 countries.

Exhibitor-list
http://www.kater.com/diskus.htm.
This is a German-language web site and mailing list of interest to exhibitors and conference organisers. The list owner is Dr Kater.

FrankelBiz
http://www.robfrankel.com/frankelbiz/form.html
FrankelBiz says it runs the web's only listserv devoted exclusively to doing business on the web, instead of talking about it. List members exchange discounts, offer business leads and do business with each other. Sponsors offer products and services at discounts to members. The list is free, moderated by a web commerce columnist, Rob Frankel, who is also a columnist for Ziff Davis' *Internet Computing* magazine.

GB Internet Marketing
subscribe@digitalnation.co.uk
The GB Internet Marketing Discussion List deals with all aspects of internet marketing relevant to the UK. You can subscribe by sending a blank email to the address above.

Global Interact Network Mailing List
http://ciber.bus.msu.edu/ginlist/
GINLIST is a project initiated by the Global Marketing Division of the American Marketing Association and the Center for International Business Education and Research (CIBER) at Michigan State University to facilitate exchange of information and professional expertise among business professionals world wide. Known as Global Interact Network, the service brings together, electronically, both business educators and practitioners with an interest in international business/marketing issues. It currently has about 600 subscribers. To find out more, visit the web site or send email to: listserv@msu.edu

Global Promote
join-global_promote@gs4.revnet.com
This list is a forum for the discussion of issues relating to sales and marketing in the world-wide internet marketplace. These relate, for example, to language, culture, currencies, payment mechanisms and trade barriers, to make the world a truly single market that can be worked through the internet. You can subscribe by sending a message to the email address shown above.

GLOBMKT
listserv@lsv.uky.edu
Subscribers discuss global marketing issues in this forum. The co-owners are Doug Tvedt and Bob Crovo. You can subscribe by sending a message to the email address shown above.

Home Based Business Marketing List

HBBM-L-Request@InternetWantads.com

This is an open unmoderated list geared towards marketing discussions and issues for home-based business owners. Topics discussed include: direct marketing, online marketing, obtaining publicity, media kits, obtaining media interviews, forming business alliances, networking on- and offline, marketing at trade shows, teaching classes and seminars, book and software reviews, obtaining referrals, relationship marketing, telemarketing, niche marketing and so on. The list owner is Monique Harris. To subscribe, send the command SUBSCRIBE HBBM-L in the body of the mail to the email address shown above.

Health Care Business

healthcarebusiness@world.std.com

This is a moderated list dedicated to discussing programs that health care business professionals can use to gain competitive advantage. Participants are invited to share suggestions, questions and experiences on business initiatives that they are undertaking to improve health-care quality, decrease cost, or otherwise attract new members and providers. Discussion topics may include ideas for new services, innovative applications of clinical or financial data, or programs designed to target specific populations. Members are encouraged to explore how their own efforts will change as new types of organisation bear risk and responsibility for decision-making. The list owner is Barbara Bix. To find out more, send email to the address above.

Fig. 53. The Directory of Internet Advertising Resources is a useful reference point for online marketers.

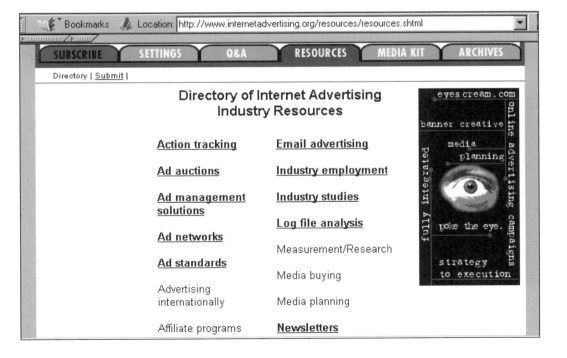

Mailing lists ....

Homebiz
http://www.onelist.com/archives.cgi/homebiz
This is a moderated discussion list for discussing all aspects of having a home business. Topics may include online and offline marketing, time management, financial management, family issues, online resources, news of interest to entrepreneurs, and money-saving tips. Blatant advertising will not be allowed including solicitations for business opportunities. This is a place to share information, ask questions and discuss common concerns. Up to six line signature files are acceptable. More than that will be trimmed to fit from the bottom up. The list owner is Bob Cortez. To find out more, you can also send email to: bobcortez@tqm-online.com

I-Advertising
http://www.internetadvertising.org/
This site is devoted entirely to the internet advertising industry: advertising sales, media planning, media buying, rich media, finding employment, campaign tracking, negotiating rates, driving customers, branding online. It runs a mailing list moderated by Adam Boettiger. This list offers a moderated discussion on all aspects relating to internet advertising, including online media planning, media buying, campaign tracking, industry trends and forecasts, creative development, cost estimates, advertising sales and other aspects relating to the promotion of a business on the internet through an ongoing new media campaign. You can visit the web site or send email to: listserv@guava.ease.lsoft.com

I-Mall Chat
listserv@netcom.com
This list discusses internet malls. To subscribe, send email to the address above.

Imarcom
listserv@internet.com
Imarcom offers a platform to learn about and participate in the further development of marketing on the global internet. It acts as a central resource to the marketing professional and a magnet to attract a community of shared interest. Imarcom is open to all those interested in or participating in marketing online. It is moderated by Robert Raisch, Chief Scientist of the Internet Company of Cambridge, Massachusetts, and others within the Internet Company and I-World/Mecklermedia. To subscribe, send email to the address shown above.

Industrial Marketing
practitioner-request@izzy.com
This list offers an environment where you can chat with people with similar interests around the world. You can be linked into a global network of marketing professionals, with a broad range of experience in a variety of industries. You can ask the marketing questions you've always wanted to ask, and have your questions taken seriously. The list owner is Prentis Hall. To subscribe, send email to the address shown above.

I-Net-Productivity
http://www.netpartners-marketing.com/
listserver@netpartners-marketing.com
The discussion group called 'I-Net-Productivity' is a self-moderated list to discuss topics relating to using the internet to improve any company's ability to market and sell on the internet. All participants are asked to stay on topic and refrain from posting commercial messages and ads, except for simple announcements. To subscribe, email to the address shown above. In the body of your email message you should write: 'subscribe I-Net-Productivity'.

International Business List
http://www.earthone.com/internat.html
The International Business List is a moderated public internet mailing list that seeks to provide a bridge between business people in all lands and provide them with a way to make contacts, find new trading partners and share resources. The site is linked to the Association for International Business. The AIB hosts a variety of free moderated email discussion groups in subject areas of international business. They are designed to help you do your job more efficiently and build an international community which currently has nearly 9,000 members. The moderator of the International Business List is Ray Gabriel. Subscription is via the International Business List web page.

Interad
interad@iponline.com
This name refers to internet advertising. The purpose of this list is to promote discussion and exchange ideas on the use of the internet for advertising. For example, discussion might include the internet and web site strategies, advertising on popular sites, and cross-media promotion of web sites. Interested participants could be drawn from advertising agencies, new media developers, internet presence providers and consultants, and corporations who are either already on the net or who are considering a presence on the internet. The list owner is Jane Jackson. To subscribe to this list, email the address shown above, with the words 'subscribe Interad' in the subject line or message body.

International-Business
majordomo@globalbiz.com
Discusses topics that concern business owners and marketing professionals as they relate to the internet and the world wide web. The list owner is Leah Woolford. To subscribe, send email to the address above.

Internet Entrepreneurs Support Service.
majordomo@ix.entrepreneurs.net
The IESS list is a discussion group for entrepreneurs and businesses doing business on the internet. The list owner is Ron Ehrens. To subscribe, send email to the address above.

Mailing lists ....

Internet-Sales
http://www.mmgco.com/isales.html
Formed in November 1995, the goal of the Internet Sales Moderated Discussion List is to provide a forum for discussion of online sales issues by those engaged in the online sale of products and services. The List publishes the I-Sales Digest, which is sent daily to subscribers; subscriptions are free. It has subscribers in Argentina, Australia, Austria, Belgium, Brazil, Bulgaria, Canada, Croatia, the Czech Republic, Denmark, Egypt, France, Germany, Greece, Hong Kong, Iceland, India, Ireland, Israel, Italy, Jamaica, Japan, Malaysia, Mexico, the Netherlands, New Zealand, Norway, Oman, the Philippines, Poland, Portugal, Russia, Singapore, Slovakia, Slovenia, South Africa, Spain, Sweden, Switzerland, Taiwan, Thailand, Turkey, United Kingdom, Uruguay and the USA. The list is moderated by John Audette, President of Multimedia Marketing Group. To join the list, send a message with any contents and subject (or none) to: join-i-sales@gs2.revnet.com

I-Shop
http://www.audettemedia.com/I-Shop/shop.html
The I-Shop community discusses topics from both the merchant and consumer perspectives. I-Shop is moderated by Will Johnston. You can sign up via the web page shown above.

ISI-L
70401.2062@compuserve.com.
This list was created by Interpretive Software Incorporated for the discussion of classroom simulation and marketing education software. To subscribe, send email to the address shown above.

ISP-Auction
join-isp-auction@sparknet.net
The purpose of this list is to support the ISP or web provider who is or has implemented auction web sites. It covers discussion about auction web site software/hardware, success tips, sharing techniques and ideas for auction web sites, and networking with each other to build better auction web sites. This list is aimed at auction web site developers, webmasters and owners, with discussion on what makes the best auction web sites successful. The list owner is Christopher Knight. To subscribe, send email to the address shown above, and you will automatically be added to the list.

ISP-Marketing
http://www.isp-marketing.com/
This web site runs a mailing list for internet service providers who wish to discuss marketing issues. The list owner is Christopher M. Knight.

JNCZ Marketing Newsletter
http://www.Information-Web.com/news/
This is a free newsletter biased towards home business in the UK: 'British Networking, multi-level marketing (MLM), home business, success and motivation for the UK.' Contact: david@information-web.com

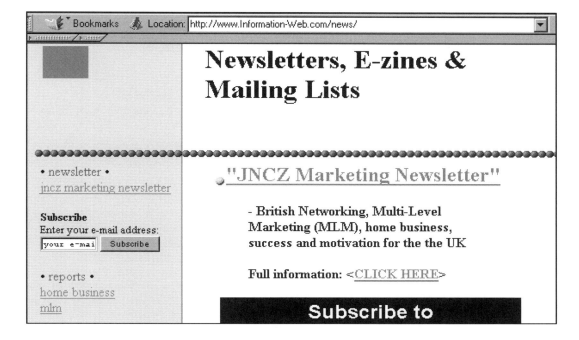

Newsletters, E-zines & Mailing Lists

• newsletter •
jncz marketing newsletter

Subscribe
Enter your e-mail address:

| your e-mail | Subscribe |

• reports •
home business
mlm

○ **"JNCZ Marketing Newsletter"**

- British Networking, Multi-Level
Marketing (MLM), home business,
success and motivation for the the UK

Full information: <CLICK HERE>

Subscribe to

Jobs-Sls

jobs-sls@execon.metronet.com

Jobs-Sls is a moderated mailing list of employment opportunities for sales and marketing jobs including advertising, customer service and public relations. No entry level positions are available. The list owner is George Smith. To subscribe, send the command 'subscribe' in the body of mail to the address above. You are asked not to include your name, address or additional text in the body of the message.

Market-ECRes

http://www.volition.com/market-ecres/

Market-ECRes is an unmoderated forum for the discussion of electronic commerce for marketing faculty, doctoral students and practitioners. The topics might range from enquiring about a research source, to testing out a new research idea. You can visit the Market-ECRes home page. To subscribe to this mailing list, you can send email to: Majordomo@volition.com with the following command in the body of your email message: 'subscribe market-ecres'.

Market-L

http://www.amic.com/

Market-L claims to be the oldest internet email list on the subject of marketing, having been in existence since 1987. The list is unmoderated. Examples of topics which might be discussed on Market-L include pricing tactics, distribution, promotion and advertising, segmentation, surveys, service quality, marketing planning for non-profits, positioning, exporting, market models, product design, marketing information systems and decision support, channel structure, relationship marketing, database marketing, marketing ethics, branding and sales force compensation. The Market-L web page includes a FAQ list. The list owner is Abby

Fig. 54. The JNCZ Marketing Newsletter is of special interest to UK-based marketing networkers.

Wool. Send email to: listserv@amic.com

Market Place

http://www.onelist.com/subscribe.cgi/marketplace

Market Place is a mailing list for trading marketing ideas, and for home-based entrepreneurs. You will be able to plug your business on a weekly basis (Fridays only). The list owner is David Hallum. To subscribe, send email to the address shown above.

MediaPlan

listserv@amic.com

MediaPlan is a discussion arena for professionals working in the planning departments of both traditional and new media agencies, and it is also for marketing professionals and academics who have an interest in media planning, buying and research. MediaPlan was established to encourage discussion of advertising media management issues. Planning, buying and media research are the broad topical areas. Discussions may cover new media, rate trends, strategic analysis, syndicated audience measurement methodology, traditional versus high-tech approaches, planning and buying techniques, information sources, planning software, media sales, reps and media computer services. The list is managed by Abbott Wool. A MediaPlan archive exists, although you must register to view it. To subscribe, send email to the address shown above.

Market Research (MKTRSRCH)

Listserv@listserv.dartmouth.edu

MKTRSRCH is an open unmoderated discussion list covering the topic of primary and secondary market research. Primary market research topics such as survey design, sample-size determination, statistical and other analytical tools, industry software, the conducting of focus groups and implementation techniques (for example, telephone, paper, personal interview, mall intercept, web surveys) are likely to be discussed. Also relevant to the list are secondary research topics such as online information databases, government information sources and other periodical research (magazines, newsletters, journals and newspapers). To subscribe, send email to the address shown above.

Market Segments (MKTSEG)

maiser@mail.telmar.com

The purpose of the MKTSEG list is to allow and encourage an exchange of ideas and information relating to advertising and marketing to target segments. These include (but are not limited to) ethnic segments, lifestyle and life-stage segments and interest group segments. Topics might include advertising creative material, media issues, research, database marketing, direct response, promotions or education relating to all the above, and other segmentation information resources. A FAQ for MKTSEG is available. The list owner is Abbott (Abby) Wool of Abbott Wool Media & Marketing. An archive exists, although you must register to view it. To join, send email to the address shown above.

Markethink
http://markethink.com/digest/
This is an all-marketing discussion list published in digest form.

Marketshare (MktShare)
listserv@piranha.acns.nwu.edu
Marketshare is a moderated list provided by Northwestern University USA, focusing on the theoretical and applied aspects of relationship marketing, brand management and integrated marketing communications. Current membership is open to anyone and includes university faculty, PhD candidates, graduate students, marketing practitioners and editors of academic and commercial publications from around the world. The list moderator is Rick Wedeking. To subscribe, send email to the address shown above.

Marketing Educator's Group
mailbase@mailbase.ac.uk
MEG is a UK-based professional association for teachers of marketing and other business subjects. The list's objective is to provide a forum for the exchange of experience among marketing educators. The list owner is Dr Stephen K. Tagg. To join, send email to the address shown above with the one-line message: 'join meg your-name-here'.

Marketing PhDs (MRKT-PHD)
listserv@vm.sc.edu
This unmoderated list focuses on topics of interest to doctoral students in marketing. The list owners are Jeff Langenderfer and David Hardesty. To subscribe, send email to the address shown above.

Marketing Teaching (MktTeach)
majordomo@hawk.depaul.edu
MktTeach is an unmoderated list for the discussion of teaching issues in marketing education. It was established by the Teaching Special Interest Group of the American Management Association Academic Council. The list owner is Robert Pitts. To subscribe, send email to the address shown above.

Marketing with Technology (MT-L)
listserv@uhccvm.uhcc.hawaii.edu
This is an unmoderated list owned by Carl Reimann and Morton Cotlar. To subscribe, send email to the address shown above.

Net Marketing
majordomo@horizont.net
This is a moderated discussion list in the German language related to all matters of online advertising, banners, web promotion and allied topics. The list is owned and moderated by Klaus Arnhold and supported by Germany's biggest marketing weekly, *Horizont.* To subscribe, send email to the address shown above.

Mailing lists ....

NetMarket-L

listserv@citadel.net

The NetMarket-L list is unmoderated. It is intended for entrepreneurs, webmasters and pioneers – anyone testing out new ideas and marketing concepts on how to promote their business, products and services on the internet. The goal of the list is to brainstorm new marketing concepts and help each other test them. Subscribers are encouraged to share ideas, make comments and suggest new marketing approaches. The list owner is Dr Leonard Manion. To subscribe, send email to the address shown above.

New Prod

majordomo@world.std.com

This is a mailing list devoted to the discussion of new product development in both product and service industries. It is intended as a means for practitioners, academics and consultants to share information, discuss and react to relevant news items and current events, publish paper abstracts, announce conferences, meetings and other events, and request advice or assistance with problems. It covers such topics as marketing, market research, management science, research and development, quality and organisation behaviour. The list owner is Bob Klein. To subscribe, send email to the address shown above.

Online Advertising Discussion List

http://www.tenagra.com/online-ads/

This mailing list focuses on professional discussion of online advertising strategies, results, studies, tools and media coverage. It also welcomes discussion on the related topics of online promotion and public relations. It encourages sharing of practical expertise and experiences between those who buy, sell, research and develop tools for online advertising; as well as those providing online public relations and publicity services. The list also serves as a resource for members of the press who are writing about the subject of online advertising and promotion. It is sponsored by the Tenagra Corporation. To subscribe, use the online form at the web site shown above.

Online-Publishers

http://www.ideastation.com/

Learn all about 'marketing with email'. This list is intended as a resource for marketers who want to use email newsletters to promote their business. It covers topics such as managing, distributing, promoting and editing an online newsletter. The list owner is Shannon Kinnard. To subscribe, send email to: subscribe@ideastation.com

Org-Marketing

http://www.amic.com/forums/

Org-Marketing aims to focus communication on the subject of marketing for non-profit and not-for-profit organisations, in response to requests from members of high-traffic marketing discussion lists. Topics which might be discussed here include low or nil budget marketing, promotion and advertising, surveys, service quality, marketing planning for non-

Fig. 55. The web site Idea Station offers dedicated resources for email marketing.

profits, positioning, market models, relationship marketing, database marketing and marketing ethics. The AMIC in the address stands for Advertising Media Internet Center.

PL2001
listproc@cyf-kr.edu.pl
The purpose of PL2001 is to discuss the use of new internet technologies by the business community. It invites academic researchers, students and members of the international business community to join in the discussion. The list is unmoderated but two individuals, Adam Krzyzek and Tomasz Sadlik, take care of it. Their purpose is to provide a space for English- or/and Polish-speaking people to meet and discuss those questions. French and Spanish speakers and nationals are also welcome, and when needed, messages will be translated into Polish. To subscribe, send email to the address shown above.

PR Forum
listserv@indycms.iupui.edu
The theme of this list is corporate and PR communications. To subscribe, send email to the address shown above.

Product_Dev
product_dev-request@msoe.edu
This mailing list is for discussing new product development. The list owner is Gene Wright. To subscribe, send email to the address shown.

Proposal-L
majordomo@ari.net
Proposal-L facilitates discussions regarding the development of business proposals, responding to government RFPs, best practices, production, marketing, contracts, training, tools and resources for planning, writing, producing and delivering proposals. The list owner is Carl Dickson. To subscribe, send email to the address shown above.

Mailing lists . . . .

Radio-Media

radio-media@adsong.com

Radio-Media is a new edited weekly email newsletter designed to combine the best of both standard discussion lists and traditional hard copy publications. All articles originate as posts, just as with listservs, but all the material is formatted by the editor. A table of contents is added as with paper publications. Radio-Media focuses on the media-planning for, and the buying and selling of, radio advertising. This includes traditional radio broadcast ads, as well as internet audio (not banner) ads. If you subscribe, Radio-Media will arrive in your box every Monday morning. To subscribe, send email to the address shown above, using the one-line message 'subscribe'.

Retail Management (RTL-MGMT)

mailserv@UToledo.EDU

The mailing and discussion list RTL-MGMT exists to enable communication about retailing and retail management practices, policies, plans and procedures. A FAQ exists. The list owner is Alan B. Flaschner. To subscribe, send email to the address shown above.

Retailer News Digest

http://RetailerNews.com/

This is a moderated discussion list for retail business owners, managers and salespeople. It is only available in digest form. The list is archived. It is published by the Retailer News Online magazine, and you can subscribe at the web site. Messages to the list should be limited to retail-oriented subjects.

Retailers Talk Shop

retailers-request@listhost.net

Retailers Talk Shop is a moderated list devoted to the management of retail stores. Whether you operate an independent store or a chain of stores, this list is intended for you. Students and educators of retail management are also welcome to join. The focus of this list is not internet marketing as such, but day-to-day operations such as merchandising, point-of-sale software, hiring issues and the like. Two types of subscription are available: single messages (up to thirty a day) or the digest version (twice a day). To subscribe, send email to the address shown above, with the message body containing 'subscribe' or 'subscribe retailers digest'. The moderator is Barbara Sybal, and the owner is Sharon Tucci.

RITIM-L

listserv@uriacc.uri.edu

This list provides a forum for discussing telecommunications and information marketing. To subscribe, send email to the address shown above.

Sales-Chat

sales-chat-request@listserv.direct.net

Sales-Chat was formed to provide a discussion forum for all kinds of people involved in selling or interested in selling – account managers,

sales reps, sales managers and other sales and marketing professionals. Typical topics for discussion include sales automation products, motivation, travelling hints and tips, success stories and horror stories, sales presentations hints and tips, selling yourself, networking, customer satisfaction, recent books, sales meetings, time management, generating leads and handling job stress. This list is not intended for advertising specific products or services. To subscribe, visit the web site, or send email containing the one-line message 'subscribe sales-chat' to the list owner, Bobbie Hartzler, at: hartzler@cris.com

Fig. 56. Are you involved with retail marketing? Then Retailer News is the web site for you. There are articles and archives, a chat room and retail forum, and you can even send electronic postcards.

Servnet
listserv@asuvm.inre.asu.edu
This is a multidisciplinary list set up to foster discussions of service in a business context. To subscribe, send email to the address shown above.

Social Marketing (SOC-MKTG)
listserv@listserv.georgetown.edu
SOC-MKTG is a list for those particularly interested in social marketing. The list is a place for those in academia, in research and in practice to exchange information to advance the field. The list owner is Alan Andreasen. To subscribe, send email to the address shown above.

Sysop-Group
listserv@property.com
The list is geared totally towards the business aspects of online services and marketing. Marketing, obtaining advertisers/sponsors and new users is its only purpose. It promises no hardware, no software discussions, 'just plain down and dirty business'. You must be a sysop or home page owner to join. This is a small list though it claims to have a high involvement rate. The list owner is Ted Kraus. To subscribe, send email to the address shown above.

TradeNet
List@TradeNet.org
TradeNet is a moderated announcement list featuring international trade contacts, products and services from around the world. The list owner is the Tradenet World Service. For subscription information, send the

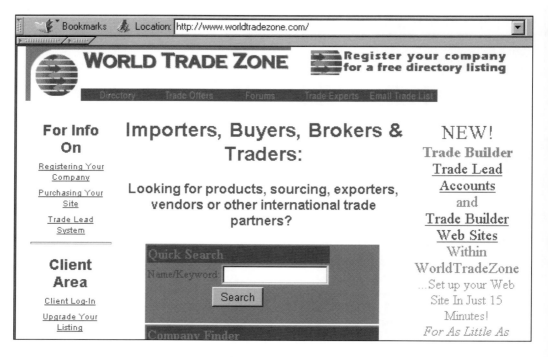

Fig. 57. World Trade Zone is a dynamic resource for marketers seeking to develop their international business.

command INFO in the body of your email to the address shown above.

Tradeshow
listproc@nevada.edu
This is a discussion list about national and international trade shows, conferences, exhibitions and commercial events. To subscribe, send email to the address shown above.

Women-Talk-Business (WTB)
http://www.listhost.net:81/guest/RemoteListSummary/WTB
The Women-Talk-Business list is set up as a discussion list for business topics. It is moderated to eliminate those one-line and off-topic posts often seen on unmoderated lists. It was formed as a moderated list due to the tremendous number of women on other lists looking to eliminate those types of posts. It focuses on business topics, and is open to anyone, although it primarily targets women.

WTZ-Intradeleads
http://www.worldtradezone.com/
This is an unmoderated international trade leads list. It is strictly limited to the posting of 'buy/sell/seek/company profile' type announcements for products and services in international trade. The list has several thousand subscribers from over 100 countries. On an average day, the list will receive and redistribute 40 to 60 trade lead posts from subscribers. Its search tools give you instant access to contact information and product offerings for some 200,000 companies world wide which are already contained in its directories, many with their own integrated web sites which showcase their product lines.

11 Business Directories

In this chapter we will explore:

▶ *some of the main internet business directories*

▶ *yellow pages, white pages and blue pages*

▶ *other online reference sources for electronic business and marketing.*

. . . .

192.com
http://www.192.com/
This web site publishes white pages directories for the UK. It offers information on 20 million residents of the UK not listed in any other telephone directory. 'Feel the power of information' i-CD has licensed many of the largest databases available in the UK and cross-referenced these together to create the largest and most comprehensive database ever to be made available to the public. By offering this service at reasonable prices, 192.com aims to introduce competition to this area of the IT industry. Its aim includes the reduction of prices and improvement of the service. You are invited to register to use its 192 reverse search engine. You can search UK-Info Disk Pro Online by any field in the database (for example, phone number, street name or post code). You can buy ten search credits and get ten free. You can conveniently purchase lists online by dropping them into your data basket and tagging them for later download.

Fig. 58. 192.com is a well-known electronic UK business directory.

Business directories ....

ADF ZipAddress
http://www.zipaddress.com
ZipAddress aims to revolutionise the way you handle addresses in the USA – by giving lightning-fast access to United States postal service data – for rapid-address capture, address checking and for mailing label printing. It claims to be inexpensive, productive, and works with everyday applications like word-processors and databases to deliver the data where it's needed. The software generates full addresses from only the postcode – just add the street number or house name. It covers all the US zip codes, and more than 100 million addresses. It also has a built-in one-off label printing facility.

AFD Postcode
http://www.afd.co.uk
The company has been delivering computer addressing solutions since 1983. Its products use data taken from the electoral roll, business data-bases, the Royal Mail and United States postal services to deliver British and USA addresses on your PC, Unix system, TCP/IP network or the internet. The Post Code program generates full addresses from only the postcode – just add the street number or house name.

All Business Network
http://www.all-biz.com/
This is a US service for individuals and business who do not have an existing web site. The full page directory listing can act as your home page, complete with your own URL that you can share with customers, colleagues, friends and family. For businesses that do have a web site, you can link the directory listing to your home page for added value. All information placed in your directory listing is included in ABN's *Business News*, a business press-release service provided to its users at no charge. You can search its database to find businesses by category, read about the latest news, and participate in forums.

ASKALEX
http://askalex.co.uk/
This is a directory of 1.8 million UK companies. You can search by key-word, name or town. The system is currently servicing over 10,000 searches and directory look-ups per hour. You can advertise your general goods and services, motor cars or property and insert personal ads free of charge. Each ad without an email address can utilise ALEX's free drop-a-note feature, for confidential contact between advertisers and custo-mers. Advertisers can also extend the life of their ads and hot-link them to their own web site. ASKALEX was designed, written and implemented by Miami International Limited which, despite its exotic sounding name, is based in Stockton-on-Tees.

Big Book USA
http://www.bigbook.com
This is a fantastic web site that puts basic information about more than 11 million US businesses at your fingertips. Each Big Book listing pro-vides the company's name, an industry category, address, city, state,

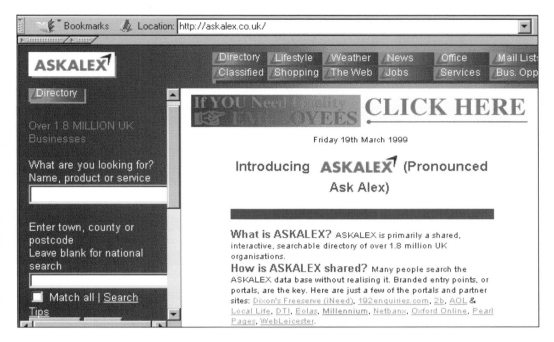

Friday 19th March 1999

Introducing **ASKALEX** (Pronounced Ask Alex)

What is ASKALEX? ASKALEX is primarily a shared, interactive, searchable directory of over 1.8 million UK organisations.
How is ASKALEX shared? Many people search the ASKALEX data base without realising it. Branded entry points, or portals, are the key. Here are just a few of the portals and partner sites: Dixon's Freeserve (iNeed), 192enquiries.com, 2b, AOL & Local Life, DTI, Eolas, Millennium, Netbanx, Oxford Online, Pearl Pages, WebLeicester.

zip code, phone number and street map location. In the classifieds section you can search ads, create ads and edit ads. It is owned by GTE, one of the largest publicly owned telecommunications companies in the world.

Fig. 59. ASKALEX offers a searchable directory of 1.8 million UK-based organisations.

BigYellow Pages
http://www.bigyellow.com/
BigYellow offers a huge coverage of some 11 million business listings in the USA. You can search this massive directory by state, business type, address and name. You can add your personal and business names to the database. The site includes a very helpful set of FAQs. The site is a service of Bell Atlantic.

Big Yellow Pages – World
http://www.bigyellow.com/g_home.html
This is a substantial compilation of *Yellow Pages* directories from around the world. It also has links to news, travel and weather information. To begin your search for the directory you are looking for, just click on a colour map of the world for the continent you require.

The Biz
http://www.thebiz.co.uk
Biz stands for the Business Information Zone. It has been developed for users seeking UK-relevant business information, products and services on the internet – whether you are in the UK or overseas. However, The Biz doesn't limit you to information on the internet. A vast amount of information, and many organisations, do not yet appear on the internet, so The Biz also directs you to these by means of its extensive and specially developed database listings. These are arranged in a clear and logical structure for quick access. At every stage you can select a full list of entries or choose by county or region. Alternatively if you know who

Fig. 60. This is the home page of BigYellow's European division. You can search by topic, by country, or by name or email address of individuals or businesses.

you are looking for, simply select the first letter of their name from the A to Z list within the appropriate section.

Business Database
http://www.ypbd.co.uk
The Business Database from *Yellow Pages* is a UK leader in location-based data. With over 11 years' experience in the direct marketing industry, it has helped thousands of companies to generate new business leads. It claims to be the UK's largest and most comprehensive single source of location-based business information, with some 1.7 million UK businesses listed. They say: 'Register today, select your target market and let us give you a count on your potential customers and show how little it costs to generate new leads and hit your sales targets.'

City 2000
http://www.city2000.com/
City 2000 describes itself as a type of co-operative. All the advertisers are grouped together in one place, so that publicity generated by City 2000 benefits all these advertisers. All advertisers are allocated their own web address, which they can use and promote in their media adver-

Fig. 61. The Biz is another UK directory which is becoming increasingly well known. It contains short descriptions and links to all kinds of organisations, categorised by industry or activity.

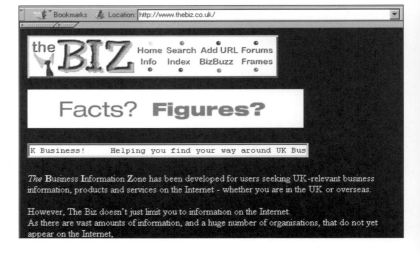

tising. Anyone accessing an advertiser's page directly from this address can then jump to the City 2000 home page and view the rest of the site. The advertisers are grouped by commercial category – everything from beauty to legal services – or you can view a complete A–Z index. It has some particular expertise in the travel industry.

City Pages
http://www.citypages.co.uk/
Based in London, City Pages is a UK-based directory of commercial links. It is designed to offer access to all the web resources of companies, products and services available in any particular area. With information categorised by postal code areas, the user simply chooses a region and postcode to narrow the search to a particular area. For example, to go to City Pages Cardiff they would choose Wales from the regional map and then Cardiff (CF) from the list. This leads to City Pages Cardiff, listing everything from leisure to property. City Pages has area offices throughout the UK. It offers to design a web site for your organisation and promote this world wide on the internet.

Database America
http://www.databaseamerica.com/
You can get an instant mailing list count for all types of US businesses, and order online after viewing sample records. You can select by industry, geographical area, number of employees and sales volume. There is also a white pages database where you can look up people by name, anywhere in the USA, and get their home addresses and phone numbers.

Datagold
http://www.datagold.com/
Based in Bristol, Datagold says its search engine is the largest of its kind on the web, with more than 35,000 sites categorised under over 100 headings. It also operates some industry specific directories covering a total of 130,000 companies. There are online searchable databases for advertising, marketing, aerospace, accountancy, computers, engineering, law, human resources, printing and packaging. Its databases are also available on CD-ROM.

Dow Jones Business Directory
http://businessdirectory.dowjones.com
This is a substantial database of US and international organisations. Dow Jones editors evaluate the web sites in the database using four criteria: content, speed, navigation and design. A site gets a score of between one and 10 in each category. Scores below five indicate that a site's performance is substandard; scores above eight indicate exceptional performance. The site looks rather like an unmoderated business magazine with links to all kinds of news, information, features and updates.

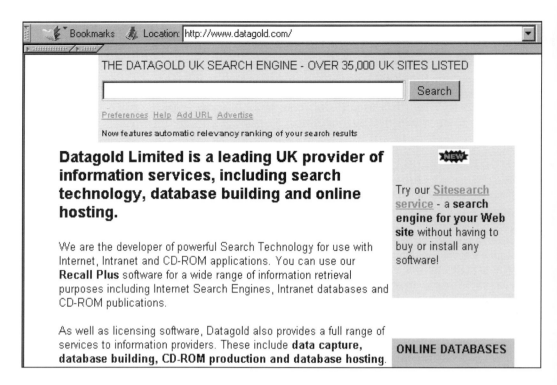

THE DATAGOLD UK SEARCH ENGINE - OVER 35,000 UK SITES LISTED

Search

Preferences Help Add URL Advertise

Now features automatic relevancy ranking of your search results

Datagold Limited is a leading UK provider of information services, including search technology, database building and online hosting.

We are the developer of powerful Search Technology for use with Internet, Intranet and CD-ROM applications. You can use our **Recall Plus** software for a wide range of information retrieval purposes including Internet Search Engines, Intranet databases and CD-ROM publications.

As well as licensing software, Datagold also provides a full range of services to information providers. These include **data capture, database building, CD-ROM production and database hosting**.

Try our Sitesearch service - a **search engine for your Web site** without having to buy or install any software!

ONLINE DATABASES

Fig. 62. Datagold is a substantial resource for business and marketing, available both via the internet and on CD-ROM.

Dun and Bradstreet
http://www.dunandbrad.co.uk/
If you're looking for information about a business, you've come to one of the best places. D&B claims to have the most up-to-date and definitive database of business information in the world. This substantial site includes a world-wide directory of some 50 million businesses in 230 countries, with name, address, line of business, company registration number, number of employees and turnover for individual companies. It can tell you practically anything you need to know about a business's financial standing, and even indicate how likely the business is to be trading in 12 months' time. As well as this, it can provide a list of all the businesses within a particular location, of a certain size, in a specific industry, and with contact names. It can show you how businesses on opposite sides of the globe are related and fill you in on overseas trading conditions and market trends. Fees are payable for full access.

Electronic Yellow Pages
http://www.eyp.co.uk
EYP links you to classified business listings in the UK. The web site gives you access to *Yellow Pages*, the UK's top classified commercial directory, and to *Business Pages*, one of the UK's top business-to-business direc-tories. You can also access *Talking Pages*, the UK's leading classified telephone information service, *YELL*, the web site from Yellow Pages, the *Business Database*, a definitive UK business data source, and *Message Services,* for communication links. EYP is a division of British Telecommunications plc.

Export Hotline
http://www.exporthotline.com/default.htm
This is a directory of contact details of businesses world-wide, interested in trading internationally. You can search or browse by product code.

Free Pages
See: Scoot.

Global Trade Center
http://www.tradezone.com
GTC provides all kinds of international trade services for manufacturers, importers, exporters, trade service businesses and opportunity seekers. You can check out its international trade business opportunities and World Trade Plan, free import export trade leads, trade bulletin board, traders' web sites and web site advertising services.

GTE Superpages
http://superpages.gte.net/
This site features a nationwide interactive USA *Yellow Pages* with comprehensive business information derived from more than 11 million listings found in over 5,000 *Yellow Pages* directories from virtually every city in the USA. This site also features the 'business web site directory' with links to over 60,000 web sites owned and operated by businesses all over the world. The site is owned by GTE, one of the largest publicly owned telecommunications companies in the world. See also Big Book USA.

GuideStar
http://www.guidestar.org/
This is a substantial directory offering a specialist coverage of more than 650,000 US non-profit organisations.

In Business
http://www.inbusiness.co.uk/
This is a comprehensive online directory of 2 million businesses in Britain from Thomson Directories, who have produced 'yellow pages' directories for many years. You can search by company, product and location. It provides a limited amount of local information. They say that details are checked and verified on average every 12–18 months. If they cannot contact anyone at the listed business number the entry is removed.

Infoseek UK
http://www.infoseek.co.uk/
Infoseek is a major internet directory and search engine. Its UK home page business link takes you to thousands of sites classified under advertising, banking, building societies, directories, employment, health care, manufacturing, marketing, news, online commerce, opportunities, organisations, property, publishing/media, resources, schools, services, telecoms, and more.

BUSINESS

Advertising
Banking
Building
Societies
Directories
Employment
Healthcare
Manufacturing
Marketing

Business directories ....

InfoSpace
http://www.infospace.com/uk/

This is the UK page for a substantial international directory of general infor-mation. It offers: location, business finder, find by category, find by name, companies online, consumer tips, local information for Edin-burgh, Leeds, Manchester, Birmingham, London and elsewhere, people finder, phone numbers, email addresses, net community, home pages, email, message boards, chat, personals, news, top stories, world news, business, fun stuff, horoscopes, international, travel guides, USA, Germany, Italy, and more. With its business finder, you can even click on a link to automatically dial the phone number of that business.

Info USA
http://www.abii.com/

You can use this site to obtain US sales leads and mailing lists, print, download or order custom lists by type of business or households by geographic area. You can obtain business profiles and credit rating codes, find detailed information about any business – employee size, sales volume, key executives, lines of business, credit code, and more.

International Business Lists
http://www.iblists.co.uk

IBL is a UK-based provider of business mailing lists. It was established in 1995 as the list rental division of the Metal Bulletin plc group of compa-nies. IBL provides up-to-date contact names and addresses of decision-making business professionals involved in financial derivatives, metals, industrial minerals, energy, shipping and mining. It can provide mailing lists to parallel the needs of any direct marketing campaign targeting deci-sion-makers around the world – in any of these multi-billion pound industries.

Internet Pages
http://the-internet-pages.co.uk

Internet Pages promotes access to businesses throughout the UK, every-thing from local builders to mechanics or carpet cleaners.

Japan Yellow Pages
http://www.yellowpage-jp.com/

Published biannually every June and December, the *Japan Yellow Pages* (published in English) includes over 28,000 listings covering hundreds of industries and businesses. With a circulation exceeding 230,000 copies distributed throughout Japan and to more than 100 countries, it has become an indispensable marketing tool and reference manual for Asian markets.

Kelly's Directories
http://www.kellys.co.uk

This is a long-established directory of 12,000 companies in the UK, giving contact details. Registration (free) is required before you can access any part of the site.

Kelly's Registration

Username	
Password	
Verification	
Surname	
Forename	
Job Title	
Position	N/A
Company	
Email	

Kompass British Exports Interactive

http://www.britishexports.reedinfo.co.uk/

You can search the *Kompass* directory of 90,000 UK exporters free, by name, product, number of employees and similar information. Basic contact details and product sectors are indicated. You can search the directory in English, French, Spanish, German or Italian. There is a discussion forum and a database of UK companies looking to appoint international agents. If you want more than company name plus telephone number, you have to register first. Some of the information is charged for.

Locator

http://www.locator.co.uk

Locator describes itself as a quick and easy way to find the nearest stores, branches, outlets, stockists and dealers of participating companies and brands in the UK. Simply enter the first half of your postcode and the name of the company or brand you are looking for and then click on search.

Marketing and Creative Handbook

http://www.mch.co.uk/

Here you can find a useful set of online directories covering advertising, design, marketing and publicity in Great Britain. You can search for information on a national or regional basis.

Marketing Information Net Directory (MIND)

http://www.mind-advertising.com/

MIND profiles the world's leading advertisers and agencies and tracks their corporate and brand presence online, collecting the widest range

The Publication

The topics within this section are...

- The Publication
- Circulation & Distribution
- Order Media Pack
- Who uses the Handbook?
- Order your copy now!

You may also wish to visit...

Fig. 63. MIND, the Marketing Information Net Directory, is another contender in the business database field.

of marketing information across 60 countries, through the most comprehensive collection of links to relevant external resources. There are literally thousands of links to the top companies, their brands and their advertising agencies, plus financials, current and historical marketing news. The information is presented in a marketing and advertising context. Its profiles put the world's leading advertisers and agencies into focus for you. What else does the company do? How did it originate? What other brands does it own? How is it performing in the market? With what other businesses is it affiliated? Full access to profiles is only available to subscribers, but you can sample a recent company profile here.

Media Post
http://www.mediapost.com/
Media Post is an advertising and media interactive directory. It aims to help busy ad/media professionals organise and communicate via email and web-based fax, with contact and list management facilities, and a comprehensive industry directory.

Scoot
http://www.scoot.co.uk
Based in Oxford and London, Scoot offers a fast and friendly approach to finding information. Whatever you need to know, you can call free on 0800 192 192. It can give information about a large number of UK businesses and services, 24 hours a day, 365 days a year. Free Pages was set up in 1992 to provide electronic directory services to UK and European markets. You can search through 1.6 million records (this number is growing rapidly), with over 3,000 business categories and 27,000 locations in its database. You can search either by name or by location and sector. There is also Scoot Holland and Scoot Belgium. Virgin Net subscribers can also reach Scoot's information service through a special icon on their home pages. You can subscribe your business to Scoot, which is seeking to take a lead in dial-up information services. You can add your business details to its database by filling in the submission form, but to guarantee that your name will be read out by its telephone

Fig. 64. Scoot offers a handy searchable business database for the UK, and for several other countries.

Fig. 65. The TelDir web site – an amazing resource where you can quickly find and start using electronic *Yellow Pages* for almost every country in the world.

operators, you must subscribe.

SearchZ
http://www.searchz.com/index.shtml
This is a very useful search engine and directory dedicated to marketing information. It covers such topics as advertising management, banner campaigns, banner design, branding, creative content, direct marketing, international agencies, international online marketing, marketing research, media buying, media selling, pricing models, privacy and sponsorship.

Telephone Directories on the Web
http://www.teldir.com/
This site claims to be the internet's original and most detailed index of online phone books, with links to *Yellow Pages*, white pages, business directories, email addresses and fax listings from all around the world. Telephone Directories on the Web was created by Robert Hoare in September 1995, and has been frequently updated since. This site apparently now gets more than half a million page views every month.

Teletext Web Guide
http://www1.teletext.co.uk/business/
There is lots of stuff here on UK business news, plus sport, weather, holidays, TV and entertainment. You can also use the site to enquire about advertising on Teletext.

Thomson Directories
http://www.thomson-directories.co.uk/
Thomson *Yellow Pages* introduced *Yellow Pages* to the UK in 1966 as sales agents for the Post Office. In 1980 the company recognised a need in the local marketplace for a local directory. Thomson Directories Ltd set up as an independent directory publisher and piloted local directories in six regions. National rollout of the *Thomson Local* followed in 1981. Today Thomson Directories delivers information products using its regularly updated database of more than two million business listings. On

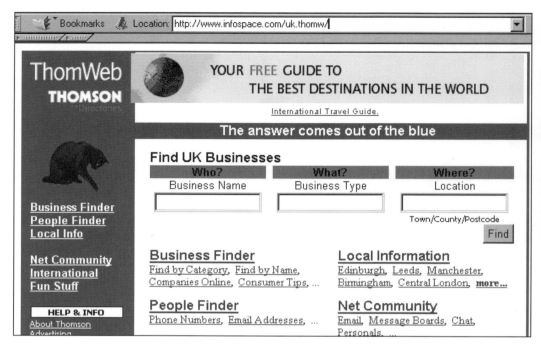

YOUR FREE GUIDE TO
THE BEST DESTINATIONS IN THE WORLD

International Travel Guide.

The answer comes out of the blue

Find UK Businesses

Who?	What?	Where?
Business Name	Business Type	Location

Town/County/Postcode

Find

Business Finder
People Finder
Local Info

Net Community
International
Fun Stuff

HELP & INFO
About Thomson
Advertising

Business Finder
Find by Category, Find by Name,
Companies Online, Consumer Tips, ...

People Finder
Phone Numbers, Email Addresses, ...

Local Information
Edinburgh, Leeds, Manchester,
Birmingham, Central London, **more...**

Net Community
Email, Message Boards, Chat,
Personals, ...

Fig. 66. Thomson Directories are now on the web. ThomWeb offers a very substantial basic resource for UK business.

this site you will find full details of ThomWeb, *The Thomson Local*, Business Search UK CD-ROM, Business Search Pro CD-ROM, New Connections and the Thomson Database.

UK Business Net
http://www.ukbusinessnet.com/
The UK Business Net aims to be a comprehensive business-to-business information resource and marketing forum. This site is dedicated to the needs of companies operating in the UK business-to-business marketplace – including their promotion to overseas organisations. It contains some 4,000 pages of free-access information on financial markets, trade news, forthcoming industrial and commercial events, trade and technical media, internet resources and more. The UK Companies Database is the latest major addition to its site. It contains contact details for organisa-

Fig. 67. UKpages invites you to add your business details to its database.

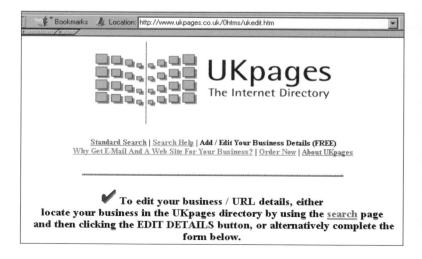

Standard Search | Search Help | **Add / Edit Your Business Details (FREE)**
Why Get E-Mail And A Web Site For Your Business? | Order Now | About UKpages

✔ To edit your business / URL details, either
locate your business in the UKpages directory by using the search page
and then clicking the EDIT DETAILS button, or alternatively complete the
form below.

tions operating in the UK business-to-business marketplace with an established internet presence. If your company operates in the business-to-business sector you are invited to take advantage of this service.

UKpages
http://www.ukpages.co.uk/

UKpages is an extensive internet directory listing of businesses in England, Scotland, Northern Ireland and Wales with direct hotlinks to web sites. It provides a free entry for all businesses in the UK and includes up to four free specialist category headings.

UKPlus
http://www.ukplus.co.uk/

UKPlus is an annotated, searchable directory of UK web sites, designed to help you find what you want, quickly and easily. It has built a vast store of web site reviews supplied by a team of journalists. Although it concentrates on UK web sites of all kinds, it includes many from all over the world which are likely to be of interest to British-based readers. In reviewing each new web site it seeks to exclude offensive material. The parent company of UKPlus is Daily Mail & General Trust – owners of *The Daily Mail, The Mail on Sunday, London Evening Standard* and various UK regional newspapers.

UK Web Directory
http://www.ukdirectory.com/

This directory lists over 15,000 UK web sites, grouped by sector. It also maintains a section for personal home pages. UK Directory offers one free basic listing to all web sites originating in the United Kingdom. Pro-

Fig. 68. UKPlus, another contender in the online business information market.

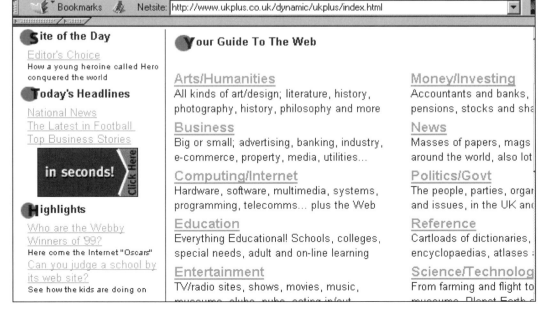

fessional banner advertising can build your site traffic and several packages are now available for web sites wishing to target a predominantly UK market. Selected fixed spots are also available on static pages within the directory to further target your exposure. It can target your advertisement campaign by serving banners according to the day of the week, time of day, user domain and category. Banners can be linked to search words so that your banner is shown when users enter the appropriate keyword. It can even exclusively target UK viewers so your banners only get British exposure. Their advertising rates are set out comprehensively and clearly.

World Pages
http://www.worldpages.com/
World Pages is an internet business directory, offering direct access to 112 million US and Canadian white pages and *Yellow Pages* listings, 9 million email addresses, 30 million URLs, and links to over 200 directories world wide.

Yahoo!
http://www.yahoo.co.uk/Business_and_Economy/
Yahoo! is the leading internet directory, used by millions of people every day. This section has links to UK business libraries, business opportunities, business schools, classifieds, companies, consortia, consumer economy, conventions and conferences, co-operatives, courses, economic indicators, education, electronic commerce, employment, ethics and responsibility, finance and investment, free stuff, history, intellectual property, international economy, labour, law, magazines, management science, marketing, news and media, organisations, quality standards, real estate, small business information, statistics, taxes, technology policy, television, trade, transportation, usenet and web directories.

Fig. 69. Yahoo! is the leading internet directory, used by millions of people every day.

12 Web sites for marketing

This chapter offers a number of starting points for:

▶ *announcing your web site name to search engines and databases*

▶ *banner advertising and link trades*

▶ *classified advertising online*

▶ *newsgroups and newsgroup promotion*

▶ *franchise marketing*

▶ *links promotion*

▶ *marketing information and advice*

▶ *setting up an online shop*

▶ *general online marketing services.*

Some words of warning

Here are some guidelines to keep in mind when dealing with advertising and marketing companies offering their services on the internet:

1. **Credibility** – If it sounds too good to be true, it probably is. Companies may default on payment promises, or change their terms of business with little notice.

2. **Identity** – Beware of strangers. Don't do business with a company that will not disclose its street address, phone number and the names of the principals. Check whether the information you receive matches that in the company's domain name registration (search out details on the Nominet and Internic web sites).

3. **Contracts** – Carefully check and print out any web pages containing payment and other terms and conditions. Don't sign or accept any contract that includes terms unacceptable to you. Walk away or take legal advice if necessary. Make sure that key terms in a contract are defined so that you fully understand them. For example, what exactly counts as an 'impression' or 'click-through'?

4. **Payment** – Don't bank on it! Advertising and marketing companies are notoriously late payers, and may not pay at all.

5. **Spam** – Have nothing to do with 'spamming'. Some companies promote their networks by disseminating unsolicited commercial email. If you reward them by doing business with them, you will receive a flood of spam yourself.

Be watchful in your business dealings online, but keep a positive outlook. There is no doubt that the internet is a very fast growing and exciting new business environment, and top commercial companies all over the world are taking advantage of it to market their products and services. Some of the internet-based names you may be unfamiliar with today could well turn out to be the blue chips of tomorrow.

Announcing your web site name

AddURLs
http://www.addurls.com/
Registration of your URL here is free of charge. You may only submit one page from your web site. They say that subsequent submissions from the same URL will be ignored.

Art of Business Web Site Promotion
http://deadlock.com/promote/
Jim Rhodes' source of free tips and secrets for registering your site at the top of the search engines, including a general marketing guide. There is also a discussion forum where you can get answers to your questions.

FreeLinks
http://www.freelinks.com/
FreeLinks is a useful guide to free web site promotions, search engines and directories, and webmaster tools and resources. The site categorises databases, search engines and links pages where web sites can be listed for free.

Hitbuilder
http://www.hitbuilder.com/
Hitbuilder's URL submission and advertising service says it posts to more than 1,000 search engines, directories and indexes. Using the top eight

Fig. 70. FreeLinks is one of many similar web sites offering to help you market links for cash.

search engine meta templates, your site can get noticed for $100. It also offers free re-submission after six months and includes a full report that shows where the site was successfully registered. DIY submission links for those who do not want to pay the fee can be found in a Free Stuff box. You will also find cheap and free resources for web site building, advertising and promoting in the links area.

How to Announce Your New Web Site
http://www.ep.com/faq/webannounce.html
This site contains some useful pages of advice for beginners.

How to Publicise a Web Site
http://www.samizdat.com/public.html
This site is well worth checking out. It contains some detailed, practical and very sensible advice by Richard Seltzer on all aspects of publicising a web site. The text matter is the sixth chapter of a book entitled *The Social Web*.

Netpost
http://www.netpost.com
Eric Ward's site offers professional awareness building for significant web site launches and events, announcements of web content launches, holistic, vertical URL submission plans and campaigns, and web news sharing with the right online people and places.

PostMaster
http://www.netcreations.com/postmaster/
PostMaster is an established web-site announcement service. You can use its online application to submit your information to 340 search engines, directories, what's new, what's cool and media outlets, plus about 13,000 interested individuals, automatically, and with customisation. Before you can use this service, you must register by filling out the online form. When you have completed this, you should within minutes receive a password via email with instructions on how to use the system. The scale of charges is shown on the site.

ALREADY HAVE AN ACCOUNT?

UPGRADE

SIGN IN

FORGET PASSWORD?

Have you tried POLITICALLY CORRECT Targeted Email Promotions?

Check out PostMaster DIRECT RESPONSE!

Send direct targeted email to individuals who **ask** to receive your information! No spamming!

Register It
http://www.register-it.com/
Register It says that 85 per cent of web users find sites through search engines. They will help you ensure that your customers can find you by registering your web site with up to 400 search engines, directories and award sites. Their experts promise to give you the title, meta-tags and marketing tips to drive targeted traffic to your site.

Starting Point – Submit
http://www.stpt.com/util/submit.html
Starting Point is one of the best known search engines on the web, and you can use its site to announce your URL. It says it is always on the lookout for new sites that offer real value and content to its users. If you have a proper web site you would like to see posted, complete the online registration form. Submissions are added to its new sites section on the

day they are received, in one of 12 categories. Starting Point users vote to select a daily hot site from these submissions. If yours wins, they will send you an email stating the category and date it will be featured as a hot site.

Submit It!

http://www.submit-it.com/

This well-known web site makes it easy to submit your URLs to more than 400 web catalogues, search engines and directories so that people from around the world will be able to find your page. You can verify that you are listed with the top search engines with their free monthly reports (sample online). Prices start at $59 for one year. Its service will also let you analyse the data and create online customer lists. The site also offers free search engine tips and marketing advice.

Submit Plus

http://submitplus.bc.ca

Submit Plus offers four programs to help you promote your web site. The first is free but requires some work on your part. The second is Basic Submit, which allows you to submit your web site to their guaranteed 600 search engines at the click of a button. The third is a DIY Auto Deep Toolkit, designed to get your web site to the top of the search engines. The fourth is Deep Submit Plus where they do all the work for you and make sure your web site contents are ready for submission, including generating meta-tags and creating powerful 'doorway pages' to get you top positions in the most popular search engines. You can also draw on help to build and promote your web site, with the aid of various resources, tutorials, tools and helpful information.

Submit Pro

http://www.submit-pro.com/

With Submit Pro you can submit your site to more than 1,000 of the most popular search engines, directories, shopping malls, new site announce-ments, award sites, international search lists and many others for about $35. The site contains some very practical and down-to-earth tips on how to prepare your web site and key words for URL announcement. Submit Pro is based in Houston, Texas.

Webpage Register.com

http://www.webpage-register.com

Here you can submit your web site to up to 1,000 different search engines and directories for prices from $29 or 1,500 search engines from $39. They will submit your details to all the major search engines including AltaVista, AOL Netfind, Excite, HotBot, Infoseek, Lycos, Magellan, Northern Light, Planet Search, Web Crawler and Yahoo!. You can take an annual service and four quarterly submissions for the price of two. You can also order a special 'Yahoo! submit' program so that your site will be continually resubmitted to this important search engine until you get a listing.

Zdot
http://zdot.com/Welcome.html
Zdot offers to professionally promote your web site. It will submit your web site to 1,000 submission locations, including hand-submitting your site to the top 20 search engines, the ones that really matter. To ensure that your web site is submitted to the most up-to-date submission locations, it updates its database daily to help ensure that bad links are removed. On any given day it says it may remove 40 submission locations and add 70, or vice versa.

Banner advertising and link trades

123 Banners
http://www.123banners.com/
This is a free public service designed to help web sites advertise each other. The concept is simple: by joining, you agree to display advertising banners for other members, and they agree to display banners for you. You can decide what type of sites to advertise on, and what ads to carry yourself, so they say you don't need to worry about inappropriate material suddenly showing up on your pages.

Ad-Xchange
http://www.ad-x.com/
This is an advertising network that lets you exchange free banners and target your viewers. It works with the AddURL submission site to create a free promotion system.

Banner Ad
http://www.banneradnetwork.com/
Whether you are big business or small business, a net community or personal page owner, Banner Ad offers to provide any web site with the traffic and added communication power it needs. The site will help you design a banner, expand your business, make your page easier to find with a free listing in a business park directory.

Banner Exchange
http://www.bannerexchange.com/
When you register you agree to show banners on your site. Each time a banner is displayed on your site you receive half a credit. For every full credit you accumulate they will show your banner once on the Banner Exchange network of web pages. The service is free.

Bannermedia
http://www.bannermedia.com/
Bannermedia offers a network of partner sites. You can buy targeted advertising through the site or even conceivably earn money for your own web efforts.

Bannerswap
http://www.bannerswap.com/
'Getting your banner ads on the web has never been easier. All you need

is a web site and a banner. By registering, you agree to advertise another member's banner on your web site.'

Banner Women
http://www.bannerwomen.com/
This is an alliance formed to strengthen the presence of women's content online. It aims to bring together different web sites targeted to a woman's audience. For members of the Banner Women network this means being able to promote your women-focused site on other sites oriented towards women. For advertisers, Banner Women offers a single media buy designed to reach any or all of the sites within the Banner Women network.

Click2Net
http://www.click2net.com/
Click2Net is a provider of targeted advertising solutions. It says its network provides all the tools needed to run a targeted advertising campaign and the statistics to analyse its performance. Click2Net handles the administration of sales, billing, reporting and ad delivery.

ClickThrough
http://www.clickthrough.ca/
This Canadian company delivers targeted advertising on the internet, and says it has contracted with hundreds of web sites, representing a vast population, largely in Canada. It has over 1,400 sites in its portfolio, including well-known names such as *Reader's Digest*, *The Toronto Star* and other leading clients.

ClickTrade
http://www.clicktrade.com/
ClickTrade (from LinkExchange) is a service that enables web-site owners to set up and run their own link partner programs. To use the service, web-site owners sign up as members. You can then use the service as advertisers for rewarding links; you can use it as link partners to earn revenue for placing links; or you can use it as both advertiser and

Fig. 71. ClickTrade is based on the idea of swapping links with other web sites.

link partner. Advertisers can choose how much to offer link partners per click, which advertisers to link to, and which type of link to include on their sites (text, button or banner). Link partners receive a reciprocal link through ClickTrade's partner tracking and display button.

ClickZ
http://www.clickz.com
As well as offering links, the site contains a fair number of articles, tips and features on various aspects of web-site design and promotion.

DoubleClick
http://www.doubleclick.com
DoubleClick delivers highly targeted advertising on the internet. This prominent organisation has a vast database of internet user and organisation profiles, which allows advertisers to target their ads by selecting from a wide range of criteria. DoubleClick aggregates and represents a large number of ad-based web sites. When a user accesses a web site that is a network member, DoubleClick dynamically displays the ad banner that best matches the user's or organisation's profile. This allows advertisers to conduct a highly targeted and cost-effective internet advertising campaign. Web sites that want to display ad banners must first join DoubleClick. It includes networks for the UK, Canada, Australia, Latin America and Scandinavia.

Four Corners Effective Banners
http://www.whitepalm.com/fourcorners/
The site offers information on how to make a more clickable web banner advertisement, improve your click-through ratios (CTRs), build advertising, impressions, link swapping and exchanges, free design tips, and more.

IntelliClicks
http://www.intelliclicks.com/
IntelliClicks offers a comprehensive set of options and features to help you promote your web site and gain maximum visibility. It claims to be the first free banner exchange network to offer the ability to include sound effects with your banner ad. The sound clip(s) are played when a visitor moves their mouse over your banner. This is designed to increase your click-through rate by stimulating the visitors' visual and auditory senses simultaneously.

InterLink UK
http://www.interlinkuk.com
Here is a UK-based resource offering free exposures, daily statistics, IP/URL tracking, and more. It claims to have two million banner exposures a month with over 3,000 members. The site is a project of Global Gold Network.

LinkExchange
http://www.linkexchange.com/
LinkExchange is another top name in internet marketing. It was formerly

Fig. 72. LinkExchange seems to have emerged as the leading name in the fiercely competitive links promotion market. Naturally, almost everything you can see on its own home page is a link to something.

a co-operative of some 70,000 smaller specialist sites, which went commercial in November 1996. Today, with more than 200,000 active members displaying millions of ad impressions per day, LinkExchange claims to be the web's largest advertising network. Its mission is to help web sites promote themselves, and to foster a co-operative community of web-site owners who benefit from the collective strength of LinkExchange membership. Members show ads for other members, and for paying sponsors, in return for in-kind advertising and various additional services.

Link Media
http://www.linkmedia.com/network/
Link Media Network provides a banner exchange program with other web sites.

LinkShare
http://www.linkshare.com/
This is another affiliates program for links sharing.

Mark Welch's Web Site Banner Advertising Directory
http://www.markwelch.com/bannerad/
This userful directory compiled by Mark J. Welch contains links to more than 500 sites featuring in-depth coverage of advertising networks. You can also use the site to explore web-site monitoring services and software, interactive marketing and advertising agencies.

Microscope
http://www.microscope.com
Microscope puts a banner (or banners) through the paces of an actual campaign. Each week a different guest media planner practises their

craft before an audience of colleagues, and the campaign is analysed and appraised. The aim is to help educate the industry in how to use and buy interactive ads.

Smartclicks
http://www.smartclicks.com/
Smartclicks says that it offers automatic targeted banner advertising where your ad will be most successful. After registering, you log in and define the types of sites on which you want your ad displayed. Then you add HTML to your page to display banners, following step-by-step instructions. Finally you create and submit your banner ad for display on the network. Within 72 hours they say they will begin displaying your ad on the network. Smartclicks is based in Charlotte, North Carolina.

ValueClick
http://www.valueclick.com/
ValueClick is a 'pay-per-click-through' advertising network. They say its program allows its business clients to advertise their web sites with no risk, paying only for actual visitors who view their site. 'No matter how many times your banner is seen, you pay only when a user actually reads your ad and clicks through to your web site.' ValueClick has offices in the United States (Santa Barbara, California) and Japan.

Classified advertising

Admatic
http://www.admatic.com
This is a resource for free classified advertising. The site was undergoing development when reviewed.

Classified Warehouse
http://www.classifiedwarehouse.com/
Classified Warehouse, from AdOne Classified Network, offers classified advertising for employment, automobiles, transportation and property for sale or rent.

LOOT: The Free-Ads Paper
http://www.loot.com
This is a free UK-based classified advertising service for private advertisers. It claims to publish more than 300,000 ads each week. It covers home and family, sound and vision, accommodation and property, on the road, recruitment and education, office, business and computers, holidays, sport, health and hobbies. Free ads received before each deadline should be published in the next available edition. Personal searching for ads is free but some services require you to register.

Net Trader
http://www.nettrader.co.uk/
This is another UK-based online classified advertising magazine, with an attractively presented home page. Click on the clear icons to view classified adverts and articles for sale by owners from around the world, or place your own free classified ad.

Web sites for marketing ....

Franchise marketing

Franchise Business
http://www.lds.co.uk/franchise/
Published by The Franchise Business in Poole, Dorset, this site includes information about UK franchise opportunities, and provides details of specialist lawyers and consultants. If you are considering the purchase of a franchise, or seeking advice and assistance regarding the franchising of an existing business, these pages will prove a useful source of information.

Franinfo.co.uk
http://www.franinfo.co.uk
Franinfo describes itself as the UK's most comprehensive directory of franchises with essential information for franchisees and franchisors. It includes useful links to all the key organisations, trade associations and media in the UK franchising industry.

Newsgroups and newsgroup promotion

Advertising on Usenet
http://www.danger.com/advo.html
How to do it, how not to do it – an explanation of why indiscriminate advertising in usenet is frowned upon. The site suggests ways in which those who need to advertise in usenet can do it non-destructively.

Blacklist of Internet Advertisers
http://www.cco.caltech.edu/~cbrown/BL/
This service is designed to curb inappropriate advertising on usenet and via junk email (spam). Don't get your web site listed here!

News:alt.www.marketing
This is a newsgroup dedicated to marketing issues.

Online marketing information and advice

Free in Cyberspace
http://www.smithfam.com/begin.html
The site aims to offer everything you need to operate your home business online. This site is full of promotional resources for web developers and designers. There are virtual libraries and internet marketing and search engine information, free articles and tutorials, web authoring and internet services. These resources are available to answer your questions and to educate the self-starter. 'We all have to start somewhere. When you are new to internet marketing or new to home-based business in an information age, you have specific questions and it's hard to find answers.' If you have a business you want to promote on the internet, you can use this site to create your own page and have it on the internet free. The rest of the site offers all the tools and resources in a DIY format, together with access to an online newsletter called *Internet Marketing*.

Free Well at Icemall
http://www.icemall.com/free/free_marketing.html
This site offers free marketing tips and reports, web marketing and search engine tactics, a free internet marketing report, free internet marketing tips, and internet marketing software with a trial download.

Freepromo.cjb.net
http://freepromo.cjb.net
Invites you to learn how to promote your site here.

i-Marketing Services
http://www.imarketingservices.co.uk
This is the web site of Sara Edlington, the UK internet marketing consultant, former marketing consultant for Demon Internet, and author of this book. Details of a free newsletter can be found here, together with a resource centre on business-building on the internet.

Internet Advertising Resource Guide
http://www.admedia.org/
This well-documented site offers a very useful information resource for internet marketing and advertising. It contains a huge number of marketing-related links intelligently categorised under main headings including introduction, planning, development, management, research and teaching. The site is an ongoing project of Dr Hairong Li, an Assistant Professor in the Department of Advertising at Michigan State University.

Fig. 73. i-Marketing Services, a web site developed by Sara Edlington, the internet marketing consultant, and author of this book.

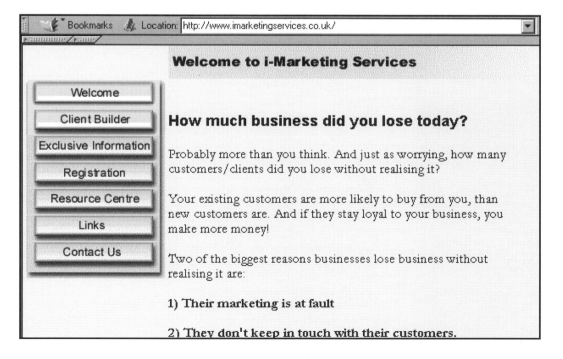

| Bookmarks | Location: | http://www.imarketingservices.co.uk/ | ▼ |

Welcome to i-Marketing Services

Welcome

Client Builder

Exclusive Information

Registration

Resource Centre

Links

Contact Us

How much business did you lose today?

Probably more than you think. And just as worrying, how many customers/clients did you lose without realising it?

Your existing customers are more likely to buy from you, than new customers are. And if they stay loyal to your business, you make more money!

Two of the biggest reasons businesses lose business without realising it are:

1) Their marketing is at fault

2) They don't keep in touch with their customers.

Web sites for marketing ....

Internet Magazine – Marketing Hot List
http://www.internet-magazine.com/hot/
This EMAP publication contains some valuable marketing background and pointers including UK market overview, market size, UK and world user demographics, and attitudes. Here you can sort out fact from fiction among the statistics about internet usage world wide. The Hot List also includes timely and authoritative information about the UK, Europe's hottest internet marketplace.

Internet Marketing Tips
http://www.marketingtips.com/
The site offers tips, strategies and secrets for internet marketing, online advertising and web site promotion for the small business or office. You can subscribe to the monthly *Internet Marketing Tips* newsletter with hundreds of promotional tips and tricks, free online.

JV Marketer
http://www.jvmarketer.com
Here is a very useful internet marketing resource from Greg Schliesmann. You can subscribe to his weekly free email newsletter called *Breakthrough Internet Marketing*. The site includes masses of free internet marketing articles, and a listing of hundreds of internet marketing tools and resources to help you in promoting and growing your business online. There is also a discussion forum where you can ask questions, give advice and meet other internet marketers online.

Market Start
http://infowriter.com/mkt.html
'Real success on the internet comes from doing lots of little things exactly right. We invite you to get our free report *What Every New Business Must Know About Marketing Online.*'

Marketing Tips
http://www.marketingtips.com/tipsltr.html
This site brings an aggressive approach to all aspects of internet marketing. You can find out about web page promotion and design, online services, online classified ads, newsgroup promotions, promotions through discussion lists and newsletters. There is also information on bulk email, auto responders, bulletin boards, electronic malls, ranking at the top of search engines, sales strategies, creating killer copy, banner ads (tips and tricks), and completely automating your business. You can subscribe to the monthly *Internet Marketing Tips* newsletter, with hundreds of promotional tips and tricks, free online.

Marketing Manager's Plain English Internet Glossary
http://www.jaderiver.com/glossary.htm
Here you can check out the meaning of web and web-design terms from the marketing manager's point of view. You will find everything here from 'hit' to 'browser wars'.

Marketing UK

http://www.marketinguk.co.uk

Here is another very useful site for UK marketing information and advice, which aims to help marketing executives be more effective. It deals with everything from the basics of marketing to setting up a web site, with links to best practice, books and magazines, marketing training, planning, marketing checklists, contact databases, public relations, using the internet, internet services, your own site, ten-point strategy, and check your site.

MouseTracks

http://nsns.com/MouseTracks/

This informative site has interesting pages on all kinds of topics from electronic transactions and digital cash, to net demographics, site design and security. There are useful lists of online publications oriented toward marketing and business, and links to forums and internet mailing lists.

PR2

http://www.pr2.com/

This site offers a free email-based course on web-site promotion. The owner, Edwin Hayward, says, 'Warning! I will be blunt about poor site design and marketing techniques, so if you can't stand criticism it's probably better to bail out now. Along the way, I will temper my remarks with a dash of humour... but I will not lose sight of your goal and mine: success on the web.'

Fig. 74. The web site PR2 offers help on how to promote your business web site.

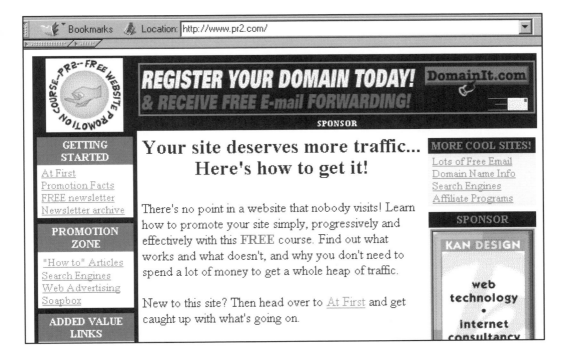

Web sites for marketing ....

Promoting Your Page
http://osu.orst.edu/aw/promote/
This site is dedicated to self-promotion and publicity links for web sites, including search engines, directories, virtual libraries and newsgroups. Developed at the University of Oregon, its pages are intended as a tutorial and reference for effectively promoting your web pages.

Promotion World
http://www.promotionworld.com/
This site has all the free information you may ever need on promoting your web site. There are hundreds of articles, interviews and other features and resources. The site includes a 40-page tutorial covering many of the basic aspects of promotion, plus interviews with some well-known internet promotion and marketing experts.

Small & Medium-sized Enterprises UK
http://uk.sme.com/
SME WorldWide is dedicated to the small and medium-sized enterprises of the world. This is its UK section, which contains some basic business links, including those to national and governmental organisations.

Sitelaunch
http://www.sitelaunch.net/
This is an attractively and intelligently presented step-by-step guide to launching and promoting a web site, developed by Aaron Dragushan. It is full of information on such topics as: is your site ready?, announcing your site, taming the search engines, using URLs in emails, the Sitelaunch Rocket, web-site diagnostics, and the Sitelaunch Traffic Path.

Twenty Reasons to Put Your Business on the World Wide Web
http://www.net101.com/reasons.html
If you still need convincing about the internet, here are twenty straightforward reasons to develop a web presence for your business. This well-tried and tested material can be viewed in English, French, Dutch, Russian, Italian, Czech, Slovene and Spanish translations.

VirtualPromote
http://192.41.61.81/
Using a magazine-style format, this site provides detailed advice on every aspect of web-site promotion. It includes a section on understanding traffic logs, plus forums on popular search engines and directory services and how to work with them.

Web Directory: How do I Publicise My Work?
http://www.boutell.com/faq/pub.htm
Another useful set of guidance notes about web-site promotion.

Web Directory: Internet Promotion UK
http://www.internet-promotion.co.uk/
This site is worth checking out because many of the links are to UK-based web-promotion resources, in welcome contrast to the preponder-

ance of American links in the net at the present time. For example, it links to search engines based in the UK with UK content, and to specific directories of UK web sites.

Setting up an online shop

Shop@ssistant

http://www.floyd.co.uk/system/index.html

Here is a UK e-commerce system specially designed for smaller and medium-sized enterprises. This innovative British product offers full functionality, plus compliance with VAT legislation, at a low price. For around £200 it is a packaged solution enabling shopping on commercial web sites. It is designed to integrate with any existing web site. Control of

Fig. 75. Virtual Promote is another site offering lots of practical tips and suggestions for promoting your web site more effectively. You can subscribe free to its email *Weekly Gazette*.

Fig. 76. The Internet Promotion Directory is a UK-based service, with links to UK providers of banner and link exchanges and other online marketing services.

147

page design remains with the site developer, whilst customisable ready-made pages are provided for order review and final order placement. To enable transactions, a range of credit/debit card, bank transfer and 'cash' payment options are included. Fully secure online payment systems and an online merchant service are conveniently integrated into the package, and a card data collection script is provided with the system. The developer is based in Hook, Hampshire.

General marketing support

2Can Media
http://www.2canmedia.com/
This is an interactive media company which aims to serve the online advertising community – publishers, advertisers, media planners, buyers and direct marketers. It operates an unduplicated, site-focused sales strategy fuelled by industry experience in advertising sales, representation and ad-management technology. 2Can says it understands that representing media publishers and web sites as individual properties is the most effective means of maximising sell-through and increasing revenue.

24/7 Media Online Advertising Network
http://www.247media.com/
The 24/7 Network has 14 affinity content channels comprised of brand-name sites that can showcase your marketing message. It has assembled a network of familiar brand-name sites designed to appeal to large and diverse audiences.

ADHunter
http://www.adhunter.co.uk
This service offers you access to classified advertising from around the UK. It covers autos, jobs and property.

Ad-Net
http://www.ad-network.com/what.htm
This is an online advertising network of member web-site publishers they call affiliates. Affiliates agree to host advertising sold by Ad-Net sales reps on their web pages. Ad-Net contracts with media sales reps all over the world to sell the available advertising space of Ad-Net affiliates to companies looking to buy advertising banners on the web.

AdNet USA
http://www.adnetusa.com/
AdNet USA claims to be one of the top internet advertising representative firms in the USA because it partners with top sites on the net. It says you can access over 25 million visitors every month through 250 million separate page views. 'Create cutting-edge marketing programs, ad banners, promotions, integrated content, and unique sweepstakes opportunities. Target audiences, identifying viewers by operating system, browser, domain, gender, ISP, Fortune 500 company, home user, time of day, geography, and SIC Code.'

Ad Resource

http://www.adresource.com/

This is a listing of web resources for advertising and online marketing support, including advertising, marketing, promotion, PR, business, commerce, articles, software and tools. The web site is a project of Internet.com.

AdSmart

http://www.adsmart.net/

AdSmart uses advanced technology to let you home in on the customers most likely to be interested in your message, based on their specific behaviours. Its TrueTargeting system claims to combine demographics and psychographics with behaviour-based targeting to help you find qualified buyers quickly and easily.

Ad-Venture

http://www.ad-venture.com

Ad-Venture is an online division of Venture Direct Worldwide, a New York-based service for over 500 advertisers seeking to drive traffic, generate leads, sales, branching or advertising revenue. The firm has fifteen years' direct marketing experience coupled with four years of online expertise in marketing, sales, planning, research, targeting, buying, creative services and reporting.

The Biz – Marketing

http://www.thebiz.co.uk/mar.htm

The Biz is a useful UK business web-sites directory. Its marketing section provides a useful gateway to a whole range of marketing data, products and services for above and below the line as well as creative services, venues and exhibitions. The marketing section covers advertising agencies, associations, professional bodies, audio-visual production, broadcast media, conferences, exhibitions, consumer marketing, corporate hospitality, data processing agencies, direct marketing agencies, field marketing, franchises, fulfilment, graphic design consultants, illustrators, mailing list brokers, market research agencies, photographers, print, print media, product designers, promotional gifts, public relations agencies, publishing agencies, sponsorship consultants, translation agencies and venues.

Community Building

http://communitybuilding.com

This extensive site will help you learn the many techniques that go into building a flourishing user community for your site.

Cyber Atlas

http://www.cyberatlas.com/

Cyber Atlas describes itself as a reference desk for web marketing. It is an in-depth business resource and another project of Internet.com.

More Advertising and Marketing Resources

Ad Resource Web Ad Primer
A good place to start if you want to understand advertising on the Internet.

CyberAtlas
The Reference Desk for Web Marketers, CyberAtlas contains market research on the Internet from a variety of sources. There is also a section on the advertising market.

Search Engine Watch
Search Engine Watch contains information on search engines for Webmasters, Web marketers, and others involved with creating and promoting web sites.

Web sites for marketing ....

Digital Music Network
http://www.dmnmedia.com
DMN Media is a network of popular music and entertainment sites, providing advertisers with access to the web's largest music consumer market. They say that, for advertisers, deciding where and how to spend online advertising dollars has meant facing overwhelming site choices, limited time and the lack of legitimate, verifiable information. Add to that the number of different ad packages, rates, terms and specs, and the job can become overwhelmingly complex and inefficient. By streamlining the entire process, DMN Media aims to deliver advertisers to their target web audience simply and effectively.

eAds
http://www.eads.com/
The company's definition of eAds means that the site that hosts the eAd gets paid based on the number of responses the ad generates, not the number of impressions provided. It finds advertisers that want to promote their products and services on the net. It then goes to web sites that have the kind of traffic that would be interested in the particular product or service being marketed and offers them a fee per response. Its staff designs and places the eAds, manages database that tracks the click information the eAds generate, and distributes month-end statements and payments to host sites.

EMAP Internet Sales
http://www.emaponline.com/
EMAP plc is one of Europe's leading media groups. It owns hundreds of prestigious consumer and business magazines in the UK, France and Germany, plus leading trade exhibitions and some of the UK's most popular radio stations. EMAP Internet Sales now offers a booking point for advertisers who want to reach thousands of UK internet users. It has signed contracts to represent some of the UK's leading ISPs' home pages which generate high UK traffic, plus quality content-based sites. It says it can offer advertisers flexible, guaranteed and audited coverage across any or all of these partner sites.

FlyCast
http://www.flycast.com/
Founded in 1996, FlyCast provides an automated real-time web advertising campaign management solutions for buyers and sellers, making it easy for anyone to buy and sell web advertising in real-time. With its Open Network, any site can instantly create a new revenue stream without incremental investment. FlyCast says it provides media buyers and sellers with real-time control over their web ad campaign planning, market testing, execution and performance monitoring.

Map Media
http://www.mapmedia.co.uk/index2.html
Map Media is a media-mapping service. It offers low-cost UK regional media-coverage maps across the world wide web. Simply create the area you wish to map, choose the format you would like it to be in

(.wmf, .bmp, .gif), and your completed map will be emailed back to you within minutes. Membership of Map Media is free. Once you have signed up you can buy as many maps, drive times and readership reports as you wish. Individual items are £15 each, or you can buy a ten-item subscription and get one item free. You can try out the service for free.

Media World (Reuters)
http://www.mediaworld.com/
Reuters Media World offers an online community for media buyers and sellers. With its News Stand service you can keep up with the latest advertising, media and brand news from industry sources, updated throughout the day. You can learn about and view samples of offerings from vendors who provide leading-edge market data and services. You can check out the featured market profile of the week – find out about media spending, consumer indices, media outlets, audience profiles and more. You can find out what's new from media industry associations: meetings, shows and publications. Media World registration is free.

Net Reflector
http://www.NetReflector.com
Design and run your own online surveys. Instant Survey is an online survey system which creates, tabulates and automatically manages most of the survey process. Net Reflector is a pay-per-response service.

New Media Marketing & Sales
http://www.nmms.co.uk
This is a UK-based sales agency offering a contact point for advertisers and media buyers looking to place advertisements across a number of audited and/or unique sites.

Real Media
http://www.realmedia.com/ Real Media
Real Media offers national and international marketers the power of local online advertising on a global basis. It has brought together trusted and high profile web sites with respected brands to form an international advertising network. This offers individual publishers the necessary visibility to attract national or regional advertising. This network of online newspapers allows advertisers to leverage the unique strengths of local information publishers, including strong local content, trusted brand identity, captive promotional vehicles, and long-term relationships with virtually every consumer and business in their markets. The Real Media network enables advertisers to use a single point of contact for placement of internet advertisements across multiple local market web sites. Real Media easily, transparently and in real-time inserts national and regional advertisements (digital ad banners) in the ad availabilities created within Real Media network members' web sites.

Web sites for marketing ....

Web Ring.org
http://www.webring.org
This completely free service offers easy access to hundreds of thousands of member web sites organised by related interests into easy-to-travel rings. You can find rings that interest you by clicking on topics in the subject directory or by using the search box. Web Ring is one of the simplest and most efficient ways to find content on the internet. Its member sites are everywhere. Anytime you find yourself at a Web Ring member page, just click on the navigation buttons or hypertext to travel to other sites in the ring. Any web-site owner can apply to join an existing ring or create a new ring. Rings are listed in the directory once they contain at least five sites.

What's New in Europe
http://www.ukshops.co.uk/whatsnew/
This is a useful source to check out new or recently updated European internet sites. If yours is a new site, you can announce it here.

Fig. 77. Wilson Internet Services. This resource is well worth bookmarking. It has been going for several years, and has built up a formidable collection of information and links to all kinds of marketing sites on the internet.

Wilson Web
http://www.wilsonweb.com
This established and worthwhile resource contains a mass of information about doing business on the net, with hundreds of articles, and more than 2,000 links to resources on e-commerce and web marketing. It has divided the practice of online selling into more than 40 different categories, and grouped materials within these topics for quick accessibility.

13 Business associations online

. . . .

American Marketing Association
http://www.ama.org/
The AMA is America's largest and most comprehensive professional society of marketers, consisting of more than 45,000 members in 92 countries and 500 chapters throughout North America. It provides benefits to marketing professionals in both business and education and serves all levels of marketing practitioners, educators and students. Founded in 1937 as a professional non-profit organisation for marketers, its purpose is to promote education, assist in personal and professional career development among marketing professionals, and advance the science and ethical practice of marketing disciplines. On its web site you can find information on the latest trends in marketing strategy, join the association, or read a sample issue of *Marketing News Online*, its members' journal.

Association for International Business
http://www.earthone.com/internat.html
AIB provides a global internet community for its members to share resources, expertise and problem-solving in international business. It provides members with an opportunity to form new strategic alliances and gain a wide perspective of commercial or cultural conditions in the many countries it serves. AIB is committed to working with and helping universities and organisations that provide training and education in international commerce. The focus of AIB is on the internationalisation of small and medium enterprises. It works in concert with government and non-government agencies around the world and seeks to exploit the value and pleasure in the interchange of information, experiences and opinions among its members world wide. AIB has 8,000 members in 160 countries.

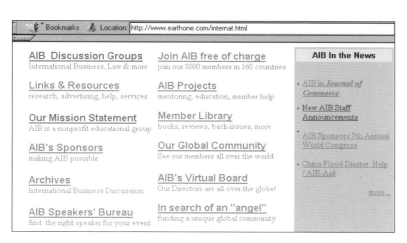

Fig. 78. The Association of International Business, a good place to keep up to date with global e-commerce trends.

Business associations..

British Exporters Association
http://www.bexa.co.uk
BExA is an independent national trade association representing all sectors of the export community. Originally established in 1940 as the National General Export Merchants Group, in 1961 it became the British Export Houses Association. In 1988, with the admission of manufacturers into membership, it assumed its present name. Membership is open to all companies and other organisations resident in the United Kingdom who export goods or services, or who provide assistance to such companies in the promotion and furtherance of export activities.

British Venture Capital Association
http://www.bvca.co.uk
The BVCA represents every major UK source of venture capital which invests principally in the UK, accounting for over 95 per cent of venture capital investment. It is dedicated to promoting the venture capital industry in the UK for the benefit of entrepreneurs, investors, venture capital practitioners and the economy as a whole. It issues a free booklet about its members, containing information on the kind of venture capital they offer.

Business Clubs UK
http://www.businessclub.co.uk/bcuk
Business Clubs UK is a federation of business clubs, groups and associations throughout the United Kindom. It is operated from the offices of Durham Business Club in the north east of England. Some 600 business networks are referred to in the Business Clubs UK database.

Chamber of Commerce Directory
http://www.chamber-of-commerce.com/
This is an international directory of chambers of commerce world wide. You can search for chambers of commerce of cities, states and provinces around the world, and find hotlinks to their web sites and email addresses.

Chartered Institute of Marketing
http://www.cim.co.uk/
With more than 60,000 members, the CIM is the world's largest marketing association. It works closely with the marketing profession, government, industry and commerce to promote awareness and understanding of what marketing can contribute to UK and international business. Its professional qualifications in marketing and sales are offered up to postgraduate level at more than 300 colleges and universities world wide. The CIM is also active in the field of competence-based vocational qualifications. Flexible programmes of residential and in-company training meet many different corporate needs, and its consultancy service matches clients with appropriate professional expertise. Its regional structure brings marketing people together to share a substantial programme of activities and services. The CIM also operates a comprehensive information service and a mail order publications service.

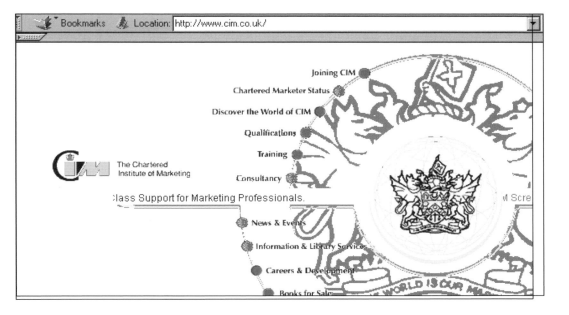

Bookmarks   Location: http://www.cim.co.uk/

Joining CIM
Chartered Marketer Status
Discover the World of CIM
Qualifications
Training
Consultancy

The Chartered
Institute of Marketing

Class Support for Marketing Professionals.

News & Events
Information & Library Services
Careers & Development
Books for Sale

Confederation of British Industry (CBI)
http://www.cbi.org.uk
The CBI is widely acknowledged as the voice of British business. Its views on all business issues are regularly sought by government at the highest levels. It represents companies from every sector of UK business from manufacturing, retailing and agriculture to construction, hi-tech, finance, transport and consultancy. If you are interested in advertising on its new site, you are invited to complete an enquiry form.

Direct Marketing Association (UK)
http://www.dma.org.uk
The DMA (UK) is the core trade organisation for all companies in direct marketing in the UK. Formed in 1992, the DMA's aim is to promote and protect the direct marketing industry. Membership includes advertisers from a broad range of business sectors, direct marketing and telemarketing agencies, and service suppliers from printers and mailing houses to list brokers and database consultancies. Fourteen industry councils create an issue-driven and focused framework for a large variety of DMA members with common interests. The DMA aims to help members by raising the status of the direct marketing industry and building consumer trust in direct marketing. The DMA (UK) is a member of the International Federation of Direct Marketing Associations (IFDMA) and associated with FEDMA (Federation of European Direct Marketers). Its headquarters are in Haymarket House in central London. There are also regional offices in Edinburgh and Leeds.

Direct Electronic Mail Marketing Association
http://www.memo.net/demma/dema.html
DEMMA offers consumers the facility for getting off email lists, as well as listing those they can join. Try some out to see how email marketing is being done.

Fig. 79. The web site of the UK Chartered Institute of Marketing.

Business associations . . . .

Electronic Commerce Association
http://www.eca.org.uk/
The ECA is a leading UK centre of electronic commerce expertise and experience. It promotes the use of electronic commerce by providing independent help, guidance, information and advice representing members' interests. It provides a forum for the exchange of experience and the development of best practice. It aims to encourage improvements in industrial, commercial and governmental efficiency by offering guidance and practical solutions to enable organisations to make the most effective use of electronic commerce.

The Event Services Association (TESA)
http://www.martex.co.uk/tesa.html
TESA is a trade association representing event organisers, promoters and suppliers. The association also publishes *Event Organiser Magazine.*

Federation of British Business Centres
http://www.tavistockdirectory.com
Over the last 10 years the use of business centres has increased enormously. They provide a convenient environment both for new business and for larger organisations wanting to open satellite operations. Listed by region for easy access, *The 1999 Tavistock Handbook & Directory* gives details of serviced and unserviced business centres and managed workspaces in the UK, mainland Europe and the rest of the world. There is a directory of business centres and managed workspaces on its web site. The Federation has about 300 members.

Federation of Small Businesses Ltd
http://www.fsb.org.uk
With some 130,000 members, the FSB is a non-political organisation formed to help small businesses. It urges all political parties to help reduce the burdens on business, to tackle the problem of late payment, and improve incentives for businesses thereby enabling them to expand their enterprise. It calls on them to deal with the problem of skills shortages, combat unfair competition, tackle crime in the high street, and ensure a Europe based on trade without barriers. FSB members enjoy a range of benefits including a legal advice line as well as information on tax, VAT and health and safety issues. It also offers special insurance against legal and professional fees, employment disputes, jury service, criminal prosecutions, and other contingencies. It publishes a regular magazine for members; and regional branches hold regular meetings for members. The site includes an online membership enquiry form.

Forum of Private Business
http://www.fpb.co.uk
Now in its 21st year, the FPB helps small and medium-sized enterprises (SMEs) to succeed by fighting for their interests in the UK and Europe, and by delivering high quality information and new products to promote self-reliance, efficiency and profitability.

Institute of Directors
http://www.iod.co.uk
The IoD is the leading UK organisation representing individual company directors. In the UK, it has 47,000 members, including directors on the boards of three-quarters of the Times Top 1,000 companies, as well as 65 per cent of members who are directors of small and medium-sized enterprises. It has impressive central London meeting facilities plus an extensive library. It also produces books explaining directors' responsibilities, including *Directors' Liabilities* and *Guidelines for Directors*.

Institute of Practitioners in Advertising
http://www.ipa.co.uk
The mission of the London-based IPA is to serve, promote and anticipate the collective interests of advertising agencies, and in particular to define, develop and help maintain the highest possible standards of professional practice within the advertising business. Representing advertising agencies accounting for some 80 per cent of UK billings, a full list of IPA members can be called up on this web site by geographic location. The information is updated every few weeks for companies wishing to contact advertising agencies direct. It also provides an advertising effectiveness databank.

Institute of Public Relations
http://www.ipr.org.uk
This is the professional organisation for people in public relations. It offers various services for both PR practitioners and businesses, including a PR consultant matchmaker service to non-IPR members. It also issues free publications entitled *The Independent Route to Practising Public Relations*, and *Winning Business with Public Relations*. There are also workshops ranging from evening sessions to two-day sessions.

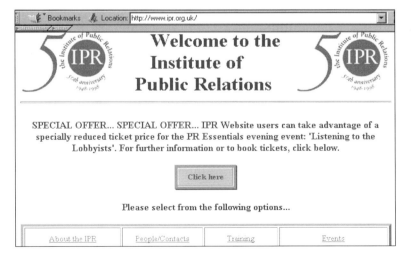

Fig. 80. The web site of the UK Institute of Public Relations.

Business associations..

Institute of Sales Promotion (ISP)
http://www.isp.org.uk
Dedicated to protecting and promoting the UK sales promotion industry.

Internet Small Business Consortium
http://www.isbc.com

The ISBC offers a productive and professional internet/web-based network to help SMEs communicate about business needs, expand their markets, share their resources, knowledge and experience. It seeks to furnish one reference source for business information, resources and experts from around the world, and protection from non-productive and meaningless side issues. This sensible and well-organised site provides help in the areas of locating business assistance, developing and establishing international business connections, offering business links, publishing a business newsletter, and providing information and news on business issues of interest. All ISBC services are free to the users.

Local Investment Networking Company
http://www.linc.co.uk
LINC promotes the National Business Angels Network, a nationwide London-based organisation which exists to match private investors – 'business angels' – with companies seeking equity funding of between £10,000 and £250,000. Its sponsors include Lloyds Bank, the HKSC Bank, the NatWest, Royal Bank of Scotland, Barclays and the Corporation of London.

14 Business media online

. . . .

Active Internet Marketing
http://www.inetexchange.com
subscribe-inet-mailer@send.memail.com
This email newsletter for webmasters, marketers and 'netrepreneurs' is published twice a week and is apparently read by more than 40,000 internet marketers. It is managed by Kevin Needham. To subscribe, send a blank email to the email address shown above. The AIM archives include a selection of articles to help you promote your web site. Some examples include proven laws of banner advertising, selecting the right domain name for maximum web traffic, the future of web marketing, tight budget web-site marketing, self-perpetuating traffic generation, getting your email marketing organised, and many other informative articles.

Ad News Online (Australia)
http://www.adnews.com.au
This is the online edition of *Ad News,* Australia's top-selling marketing, media and advertising magazine.

Advertising Age
http://www.adage.com
With offices in New York, Chicago and Los Angeles, *Advertising Age* has been a leading source of marketing, advertising and media news, infor-

Fig. 81. Active Internet Marketing, an email newsletter for webmasters, marketers and 'netrepreneurs'.

mation and analysis for more than 65 years. The Ad Age Group is a marketing partner with *Advertising Age, Advertising Age International, Business Marketing* and *Creativity*. Other brand publications and products include *Net Marketing, Ad Age Daily Fax,* the global *Daily World Wire*, conferences and seminars, events and event marketing, and custom publishing. Each issue of *Ad Age International* provides global exclusives on subjects from world-wide advertiser rankings to profiles of marketing superstars.

AdWeek Online
http://www.adweek.com/
The online services and web sites of this US media group include: Adweek Online, Brandweek Online, Mediaweek Online and MC Online. Its online premium services include definitive industry guides and directories of companies, people, addresses, phone numbers, statistics, resources, rankings and much more – for example, *The Brandweek Directory, The Mediaweek Directory, The Adweek Directory, The IQ Directory, Shoot Directory, Adweek Asia Directory* and *The Marketer's Guide to Media*.

All Business Network
http://www.all-biz.com/
You can use this web site to find businesses by category, read about the latest news and participate in forums.

Automatic ID News
http://www.autoidnews.com/
Barcodes, RF/DC and other automatic data-capture technologies are the focus of this web site through product listings, case studies and trade show lists.

BBC News
http://news.bbc.co.uk/
Use this professionally developed site to view current news stories, including some Real Audio clips. There are links to front page news, world news, UK news, UK politics, business, science and technology

Fig. 82. Ad News is a leading Australian marketing magazine.

Fig. 83. BBC News online. It includes a link to Business News.

news, health, education, sport, entertainment, talking point, in depth, on air, and archives. Material is available in English, Welsh, Russian and Spanish.

Card Technology Magazine
http://cardtech.faulknergray.com
This site examines issues and developments in smart cards and other advanced card technologies in banking, transportation, government and university settings. Articles from past issues of Card Technology can be a useful resource if you need hard-to-find information concerning a particular topic in smart card technology. Using the numbered lists provided here, you can locate the article or articles you need and order reprints online.

Central European Business Daily
http://www.cebd.com
Here is a useful media resource for companies seeking to do business in Eastern Europe. It includes daily news updates organised by sector and country. Free registration is required before you can access the site.

Changes International
http://www.changes.first.uk.com/
This is an online UK newsletter designed to help multi-level marketing distributors, and containing tips and hints. You can access its internet forums where you can speak to other users 24 hours a day. Need some help, or got a question? Someone should be able to answer it for you. Guests are welcome to browse around the site but you need to be a newsletter subscriber to enter the members' area where there is plenty of lively information and tips from all their UK top earners and retailers.

Channel Seven

http://www.channelseven.com

'The networking source for internet development - our mission is to drive the internet industry forward by shining the spotlight on business innovation and excellence and by bringing the industry leadership together online and at industry events.' Begun in 1997, this is a professional resource for builders, advertisers and marketers of internet businesses. It offers a daily analysis of what it considers the best ads and commerce on the web. It claims to have an audience of more than 100,000 internet industry executives per month, more than a million ad views per month, and over 10,000 industry members world wide. It has carried out 200 internet advertising case studies. There is a special Channel Seven Europe section.

Fig. 84. Channel Seven Europe. This e-zine focuses on e-commerce in Europe.

College Press Network

http://www.cpnet.com/

Do you want to promote your product or service to students and the educational market? The College Press Network offers a useful index of online student newspapers. You can also explore Rate Link, a service designed to help you sell your advertising space (print and online) 24 hours a day.

ClickZ

http://www.clickz.com

This is a lively source of information about marketing and e-commerce. There are articles on such topics as advertising management, banner campaigns, banner design, branding, creative content, direct marketing, international agencies, international online marketing, marketing research, media buying, media selling, pricing models, privacy and sponsorship. You can also receive a free daily email on the subject of internet marketing, either in plain text or html format.

Clue to Internet Commerce

http://www.ppn.org/clue/

Published weekly, *A Clue to Internet Commerce* is a lively and outspoken resource designed for those who want to profit on the world wide web.

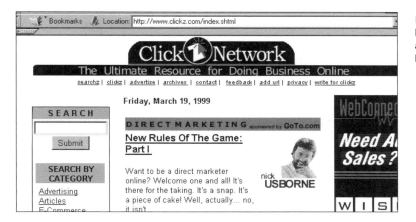

Fig. 85. ClickZ offers a lively magazine covering all aspects of doing business online.

Every week the editor gives you a quick guide to the week's headlines, telling who's got a clue – and who hasn't – based on his 20 years' experience as a business reporter.

Communications Week
http://www.cmpnet.com/search/News
CMP *Communications Week*'s guide to electronic commerce and doing business on the web, with a particular emphasis on technology news.

Dan Janal's Online Marketing Magazine
http://www.janal.com
This web site contains dozens of free articles from Dan Janal's Online Marketing Magazine. Dan Janal is an author, online marketing consultant and speaker who helped in the public relations launch of America Online about 15 years ago. You can use the site to obtain information about creating successful online marketing plans, publicising and promoting your web site, crisis communications and the internet, creating a web site from a marketer's point of view, measuring results from web marketing campaigns, protecting your company from fraud and libel on the internet, and other topics.

Daily Telegraph
http://www.telegraph.co.uk
This is the home page of the Electronic Telegraph, one of the first UK newspapers to make an appearance on the internet. The site contains substantial news, business, motoring, sports, expatriates, prestige homes and other resources.

Digital Edge
http://www.digitaledge.org
Here is a subscriber-based information site which shows the interactive world 'from the precipice', and gives you the 'digital edge' you need to compete successfully in this new medium. You can explore weekly web news, archives, hot picks and many other resources. It is a service of the New Media Federation and Newspaper Association of America.

Direct Marketing News
http://www.dmnews.com/
This is the online edition of the newspaper *Direct Marketing News*. The site includes the DM News Archive, a comprehensive, searchable database of articles and features published since January 1998. The search is free to everyone. The search results include article title, the web site publish date, and a short synopsis. To view full articles over a month old, you must subscribe. A one-year subscription costs $25, which entitles you to access an unlimited number of articles.

Ebusiness & Strategies
http://webrmarket.hypermart.net/news.htm
This site features tips of the month to help online marketers. Past examples have included: exploiting your classified advertising to its fullest, how to keep browsers coming back, profiling the average internet buyer, and advertising to newsgroups. It also offers secrets on advertising with the major online services, how to get hundreds of quality prospects to email you weekly, and how to accept credit cards and cheques by fax, phone and email.

E-Commerce Alert
http://www.eCommerceAlert.com
This is a newsletter and listserv which offers analysis, interaction and updates on strategies and tactics for electronic commerce professionals.

Economist
http://www.economist.com/
This is the web site of one of the leading UK and international journals of economic, business and political news. A year's subscription to *The Economist* in print costs £84 in Britain and $125 in the United States. This includes full access to the web edition, which contains the complete contents of *The Economist* and is published each Thursday by 10pm London time. Subscriptions to the web edition alone cost $48 or equivalent world wide. Print and web edition subscriptions include free unlimited retrievals from the archive. It is worth checking out the site for current free trial offers.

eMarketer
http://www.emarketer.com/
This is a quality online marketing magazine published by Channel Seven, with information, news and marketing chat from around the world. It is a good resource for keeping up to date with the latest trends in e-commerce and e-marketing. Recent stories, for example, included MicroSoft's Venus Project – its biggest dollar project ever – designed to give internet access to the Chinese people via television sets. The site includes some useful tracking of internet use statistics, trends and demographics.

E-News
http://www.enews.com/
This is a good place to come if you want to track down US consumer and

business magazines. You can search for magazines alphabetically, or by subject by exploring over 100 different interest areas.

Entrepreneurial Edge Online
http://www.edgeonline.com/
This is a business advice magazine offering more than 4,000 documents and advice on all aspects of doing business online. It includes step-by-step interactive modules on all aspects of starting and growing a business. These include guidance on how to establish a public relations campaign, how to establish a promotional mix, how to create a sales brochure, how to write a direct mail piece, how to create an effective advertisement, how to create a newsletter, and how to write and execute a press release.

Euro-Babel (France)
http://www.blueskyinc.com/babelidx.htm
You can join the Euro-Babel web digest and discussion list and learn more about web-related developments and advertising in Europe. The site examines similarities and differences between Europe and America – especially in terms of graphics and web design, information architecture, banner advertising, site categories and content, and new developments and innovations. Topics include currencies, e-commerce and payment mechanisms, and news about trade barriers, telecommunications and regulations. It's free, and open to anybody who wants to know how to communicate and market more effectively on the web in Europe. Just fill out the online form to subscribe.

European Business News
http://www.ebn.co.uk
EBN offers a 24-hour news channel broadcasting across Europe by cable and satellite. It provides up-to-the-minute business news, drawn from Dow Jones and written from a European perspective. For evening viewing, it offers a range of topical feature programmes on, for example, business travel, science and technology, media and culture.

Financial Times
http://www.ft.com
This is the online edition of the UK's famous pink daily broadsheet, 'where information becomes intelligence'. This is the place to come for quality national and international in-depth news coverage, analysis and comment and business, financial and market reports. For registered users, FT Online provides detailed background on more than 11,000 companies world wide, access to a massive archive of more than four million articles from 3,000 databases, plus an impressive range of research and personal financial management tools.

First Steps – Marketing & Design Daily
http://www.interbiznet.com/nomad.html
First Steps offers a broad marketing coverage including archived material. The archives are packed with over four years' interesting and useful articles about online marketing.

Online media..

Forbes Magazine

http://www.forbes.com

This is the impressive web site of one of American's most prestigious business magazines. It contains news stories, special reports, archives, celebrity columns, a guide to the world's richest people and highest paid corporate executives, and a huge number of other editorial features and business tools.

Free Pint

http://www.freepint.co.uk/

Free Pint is a free email newsletter written by information professionals in the UK. It gives you tips, tricks and articles on how and where to find reliable web sites and search more effectively. It is currently sent to more than 20,000 subscribers around the world every two weeks. This breezy and down-to-earth publication has won many awards and has been profiled in a large number of publications. Free Pint accepts contributions from information professionals for the Tips & Techniques and Feature Article sections of the newsletter. Although there is no payment for writing for the newsletter, authors may follow their article with an optional 100-word biography paragraph or promotional paragraph about themselves and their company or organisation. If you would like to submit an article, get in touch. Free Pint is published by the information consultancy, Willco.

Gator's Byte

http://www.gators-byte.com/

This is a weekly column dedicated to web-site promotion, helping potential customers to find your site, and helping you to keep them coming back. There are nine separate sections of the site.

Guardian

http://www.guardian.co.uk

This is the home page of Guardian Newspapers Limited, which leads you to *The Guardian* and *The Observer* online. You can sample a broad diet of national and international news and features. You have to register for the sites once you go past the home page and the front page headlines and news summaries. This process only takes a couple of minutes and will allow you permanent and free access to all the related sites.

Guerrilla Marketing Online

http://www.gmarketing.com/

This is a weekly web magazine aimed at small business, entrepreneurs, sales people and marketers of all kinds. 'Guerrilla Marketing,' it says, 'gives small businesses a delightfully unfair advantage: certainty in an uncertain world, economy in a high-priced world, simplicity in a complicated world, and marketing awareness in a clueless world.' The first *Guerrilla Marketing* book was published by Houghton Mifflin in 1984. Today there are sixteen volumes of this bestseller in 37 languages and more than a million copies have been sold world wide. The book is required reading in many MBA programmes throughout the world. The author, who taught marketing at the University of California, Berkeley, now serves

Fig. 86. Guerrilla Marketing, a weekly web magazine based on the best-selling marketing handbook of the same name.

on the Microsoft Small Business Council and the 3Com Small Business Advisory Board.

Hollis UK Press and Public Relations Annual
http://www.hollis-pr.co.uk
Hollis is a leading British publisher of information for the public relations, sponsorship, corporate hospitality, media, marketing and advertising industries. Its titles include *Hollis UK Press & Public Relations Annual, Hollis Europe, Hollis Sponsorship & Donations Yearbook, Hollis Sponsorship Newsletter, Hollis Sponsorship Awards, Hollis Business Entertainment, Hollis Database, Willings Press Guide, Advertisers Annual, The Marketing Handbook* and *Handy Hollis*. The Hollis Database, updated daily, offers a comprehensive source of information available on the PR, marketing, advertising, media, sponsorship and corporate hospitality markets in the UK and Europe. You can select your target audience by a wide range of criteria.

Iconocast
http://www.iconocast.com/
Iconocast is a weekly e-cast (mailing list) that provides you with web marketing analysis and news, including exclusive coverage of advertising, broadcasting and market research, written in a breezy, concise style.

Independent
http://www.independent.co.uk
Here you can catch up with the top UK and international news stories seven days a week from the UK broadsheet newspaper. The site includes a business section.

Front Page

Order Form

Free Web Marketing Resources

Reviews

Custom Help

Internet News

Who We Are

Sign Up For Marketing Tips By Email

InfoScavenger
http://www.infoscavenger.com/
If you're looking for the best web marketing strategies, sources for free publicity, and where to find out what your competitors are doing, you've come to a good place. *InfoScavenger* is a monthly print newsletter which puts in your hands every month selected web resources for free publicity, internet marketing tips and tools, powerful promotion and advertising strategies, business leads and business intelligence.

Interactive Marketing Magazine
http://www.imcweb.com/IMM/IMM.htm
Published monthly by Interactive Marketing Communications. The site was undergoing refurbishment when reviewed.

Internet Investors Journal
http://www.discover.co.uk/-iij/
This is a British-based investment magazine covering 30 stock markets (including emerging markets) and specialising in unit trusts. Its editor was a top-performing international fund manager.

Internet Marketing & Technology Report
http://www.computereconomics.com/
The report is published monthly by Computer Economics Inc, an independent research organisation devoted to helping corporate executives plan their e-business strategies and IT executives control and manage their IT costs. They also publish *Internet & Electronic Commerce Strategies*, available on annual subscription.

Internet Works
http://www.futurenet.com/internetworks/
This is one of the best non-technical UK internet business magazines. Explore the latest news concerning the UK and e-commerce from around the world wide web. Typical features include: so you want to get into e-commerce, a brief guide to the process of opening an online shop, with hints for doing it better and guidance on some of the pitfalls and problems. Internet Works has also created a web-design agency listing to help you battle through the internet mire.

Fig. 87. Internet Works is a great place to keep up with all the latest happenings on the internet.

Internet World
http://www.iw.com/
Internet World (formerly *Web Week*) provides the industry news and features that help today's internet professionals keep ahead of the competition and on top of the best vendors, products and solutions for their businesses. This is a substantial magazine, news and information resource covering most aspects of the internet, and containing a large amount of information about e-commerce. The site includes news, commentary, personality profiles, advice and site pointers.

ITN

http://www.itn.co.uk/
This is the web site of UK Independent Television News, which includes a business section. It contains ITV, Channel 4 news, Channel 5 and Euronews. With ITV webcam you can watch live pictures from the ITN news centre in London, and be at the heart of the newsroom as the bulletins are prepared. With 'news ticker' you can be the first to read about breaking stories as they happen, and see the headlines, updated throughout the day, on your computer screen. The service can stay on even if you leave the ITN web site – just click the news ticker option on the front page. ITN says it is offering Britain's first personalised desktop news service.

Journal of International Marketing
http://www.ama.org/pubs/jim/index.html
This is a journal published by the American Marketing Association. You can view article abstracts online, but access to the full text requires a subscription.

Larry Chase's Web Digest For Marketers
http://www.wdfm.com
This is a professionally presented online marketing newsletter with listings and descriptions of sites of interest to marketers. It began in 1995, and now claims to have an audience of 80,000.

MarketFiles
http://www.marketfiles.com/
This site offers a stimulating archive of marketing case studies drawn from around the world. Each case is described in the context of its marketing, planning and communications strategies, and includes the relevant visual media used during its engagement. This is a useful resource for anyone wanting to develop a marketing project, assignment or study. The site also has interactive areas specific to the members of the education and business community where you can hold discussions or post your questions and comments under the existing ones.

Marketing News Online
http://www.ama.org/pubs/mn/index.html
This is a publication of the American Marketing Association. Here you can find cover stories and insightful features from the latest issue of Marketing News, updated every Monday and Thursday.

Letters/Opinion
Current Issue
News
E-Commerce
Intranet World
Web Development
Infrastructure
IW Labs
Internet Careers
Industry
ISP World

Staff Bios
Editorial Beats
Editorial Calendar
Back Issues
Media Kit
Career Connection
Subscribe

Online media...

Marketing Online (UK)
http://www.marketing.haynet.com/

Marketing Online is produced by *Marketing* magazine for client marketers and their agencies. It includes top stories from each week's issue plus a daily news update and details of forthcoming events in the marketing calendar. It aims to help you stay aware of what is happening in the world of marketing, as it happens. Updated daily, it also contains *Adwatch*, which appears a day before it is printed in magazine format. There is a comprehensive directory of links to other online marketing services.

Marketing Week (UK)
http://www.marketing-week.co.uk

Marketing Week is a leading UK weekly news magazine for marketing, advertising and media professionals. Published every Wednesday morning just after midnight, *Marketing Week* hits the web bringing the latest news from the UK to a world-wide audience and offers a taste of what is found in the magazine.

Media Central
http://www.mediacentral.com

Media Central offers a daily and weekly selection of news, analysis, information, insight and commentary for internet media professionals.

Media Professional
http://www.accessabc.com/ympc/ympmedia.html

Media Professional is the monthly newsletter of the Young Media Professional's Committee of the US Audit Bureau of Circulation. It offers marketers and publishers news, tips, resources and job opportunities.

Media UK Directory
http://www.mediauk.com/directory/

This valuable site offers a detailed directory of UK media sites on the internet: radio, television, magazines and newspapers. In the television directory you can find all UK television stations – analogue, digital terrestrial or digital satellite – with email, links and programme schedules, plus Sky Digital channel numbers. The newspaper directory includes contacts to all national and online local newspapers, news services and resources, including press release distribution services. The radio directory contains all the UK's radio stations, and its magazine directory lists all online business and consumer magazines. This site is currently serving over 160,000 pages every month.

Media Week
http://www.mediaweek.co.uk

All the latest UK-sourced news reports about media business – cable, TV, radio, press and internet.

Net Marketing
http://netb2b.com/

This is *Advertising Age*'s net marketing journal. To help sort out the various issues and marketing areas for today's business-to-business marketer,

Net Marketing has divided the subject into eight distinct educational tracks that look at everything from setting up a web site to e-commerce opportunities. Each track offers helpful case studies, how-to articles, and pricing information designed to help you carry out the marketing function more effectively.

Netscape Netcenter Business Journal
http://home.netscape.com/netcenter/businessjournal/
Here you can download personalised business information on the web from Netscape by registering for 'MyNews'. Topics include industry news, business and finance, computing, energy, healthcare, internet and multimedia, mass media, networking, telecom, and other industries.

Newslinx
http://www.newslinx.com/
This is a daily web news service which brings you the latest topical news stories on the net. The emphasis is on stories concerning the internet – financial and political developments, web-based scandals, technical innovation, e-commerce news and internet celebrities.

News Now
http://www.newsnow.co.uk/
Based in London, News Now Publishing Ltd is a UK provider of 'news aggregation' services. Could a news feed help you market your own web site, by providing news stories and features to complement your content? Then News Now Direct and free News Links could be the answer. Check out the latest UK headlines drawn from a variety of inter-net news sources, updated every five minutes. The site includes a search facility of archived material, or you can browse by topic: business, sports, entertainment, technology and others.

News Review
http://www.news-review.co.uk/
This is an online business news review service offering summarised cor-porate, economic and business news. There is a Weekend City Press Review containing a comprehensive summary, compiled by financial journalists, of the business news from the quality UK weekend newspa-pers. The Review is available from Sunday evening by email. You can access the archive of back copies of the Review by company name back to June 1995. A large part of the archive is available free of charge. You can also do a search of the full text of back copies of *Marketing Week*, and many other leading journals.

The Observer
See *Guardian*, above.

Pangaea: Interactive Global News
http://www.pangaea.net/ign/news.htm
Pangaea is useful source of marketing news and business headlines from around the world. It is aiming to become a leading source and reference for international business, a one-stop global commerce shop for the con-

sumer marketplace and global business practices.

Paper Boy
http://www.paperboy.net/
This useful service puts together your own personal newspaper using data collected electronically from various daily news sites. You type in your key words and Paper Boy does the rest. You will then receive a list of web links delivered daily by email. You can also search online.

Periodical Publishers Association
http://www.ppa.co.uk
The PPA is the trade organisation for magazine publishers in the UK. Here you can find a comprehensive list of UK magazines on the web, useful data about the magazines, with links to the *1998 Magazine Handbook*, the latest *How Magazine Advertising Works* research report, plus an A–Z of magazine publishers.

Press Association
http://www.pa.press.net/
The PA News Centre online includes broadly based quality national and international rolling news headlines and news reports.

Pressline
http://www.pressline.com/
Pressline is a multilingual European database archive containing more than 20,000 press releases.

Fig. 88. The Press Association naturally has its own very impressive online global news service.

Publicity.com
http://www.publicity.com/
This online publication is all about publicity, the media, marketing and more. 'And if we're doing our job right, you shouldn't be able to tell the difference among the three.' It aims to keep you informed about publicity, how to get it, how to use it, what makes you look good, what makes you look bad. It also offers some of the latest on those in the spotlight and what they are doing there. Most of the articles in the archive can be obtained in their entirety simply by emailing them a request form linked to the article. So if you want to get your hands on anything, just let them know.

Research Index
http://www.researchindex.co.uk/
This is a quick and easy way to find the news reports you need. Research Index is a database that indexes the headlines of news, views and comments on industries and companies world wide, as reported in the UK national press and a range of quality business magazines. Every significant daily and Sunday newspaper, business magazine and periodical is indexed. The site is available in several different European languages.

Sales Arena
http://www.pavilion.co.uk/sales-arena/
This is a useful resource centre for sales and marketing information. It focuses on improving sales and marketing success through technology, business images and people. It contains sections on sales, marketing, design and public relations, with links to relevant services and suppliers.

Sales Doctors
http://salesdoctors.com/
'Seeking cures for the common close' – this is a weekly magazine written by sales experts to help you sell more of any product or service and keep your customers coming back. You can browse 10 to 12 new sales, service, marketing and management articles every Monday morning and view the most recent 20 issues. In Sales Doctors Interactive you can share sales leads, find or post a sales job, locate marketing resources, and seek advice from other readers.

Silicon
http://www.silicon.com
This is a quality business-information review, with daily updates and reports on the latest developments in e-commerce. Free registration is required.

Sunday Times
http://www.sunday-times.co.uk
To gain free access to the internet editions of *The Sunday Times* you are required to complete the online registration form.

Online media

Tenagra Resources
http://marketing.tenagra.com/perdesc.html
Links to internet print publications, periodicals and newsletters.

The Times
http://www.the-times.co.uk
To gain free access to the internet editions of *The Times* you are required to complete the online registration form.

UK Business Park
http://www.businesspark.demon.co.uk/
UK Business Park summarises the main news stories since 1995 – 'No nonsense, just the facts!' Its database includes over 1,400 companies. Its users include executives, sales and marketing professionals, information professionals, business analysts, investors, and others doing business in the UK. It publishes a *UK Activity Report* with sales leads and business intelligence, including information on acquisitions, new projects, expansion plans, strategy, major new products and other important developments. It is delivered to your email address every week for under £1 per week. You can take out a three-week trial.

UK Company News
http://www.companynews.co.uk/
UK Company News provides a central source for the latest information on UK-quoted company finances, products and services. The new issues sections feature regular updates on forthcoming, current and recent initial public share offers. Take a look at the Share Tracking and Ranking (STAR) bulletin which provides regularly updated UK share ranking lists enabling investors to manage their own portfolios. The service has been developed by MD Management, an independent investment advisory company established in 1986. The firm specialises in investment research and analysis and does not deal directly with individual clients.

Web Scout
http://www.webscout.com/
Web Scout trawls the internet to seek out quality sites, and then publishes reviews of them here. Its extensive index of reviews is selective, and includes only what it considers are the net's very best web sites, archives and discussion groups within various subject categories. These cover arts, business and investment, computers, education and reference, entertainment and hobbies, government, politics and law, health and medicine, the internet, news and media, people and society, science and technology, shopping, sports and fitness, travel and regional. You can receive reviews via its free weekly email newsletter. If you can't find an appropriate resource in its index, you can use Super Search to search the entire net using 30 of the web's most useful search engines, conveniently displayed in a small floating window. It has a good section on business and marketing web sites.

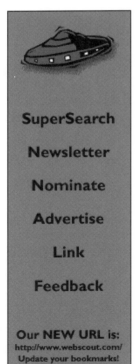

Virtual Promote Gazette
http://www.virtualpromote.com
This is a bright and well-presented promotion and marketing newsletter on the web, a weekly gazette delivered to your email box full of the latest news on site promotion and e-commerce. It is free to subscribe and you can browse through the past issues. There are masses of information on ways of promoting your web site and getting linked to search engines and databases.

Wilson's Web Marketing Today
http://www.wilsonweb.com/webmarket/
You'll find links to thousands of online articles about effective web marketing and to online resources for business on this web site. It covers such topics as analysing site traffic, associate programs, banner ads, books, branding on the web, case studies/models, classified ads on the web, customer service and chat rooms for business. There is guidance on design, demographics of the web, domain names, e-commerce, email marketing, justifying web-site expenses, legal issues, marketing research, new marketing approaches, newsgroups and mailing lists. Find out about periodicals and e-zines, privacy issues, promoting your web site, PR, push marketing, retail online stores, reviews, search engines, sponsorships, web hosting services, wholesale online sales packages and prices, turnkey web stores, and web commerce today. From its beginning in August 1995, the Web Marketing Information Center has grown into a comprehensive web marketing resource. Keep checking. New articles and resources are added every month.

Fig. 89. The web site of Wired News, a service of the well-established magazine *Wired*.

Online media..

Wired News
http://www.wired.com
Clear, concise and complete, Wired News is one of the best internet media sites. It is an essential source of daily news and analysis of the technologies, companies and people driving the information age. Going beyond traditional technology coverage, it delivers an in-depth, informed insider's perspective on how technology is affecting business, culture and politics on a daily basis. The company is based in San Francisco.

Further reading

. . . .

Burn Rate: How I Survived The Gold Rush Years On The Internet
Michael Wolff
A superb and rather scary account of one writer's attempt to make several millions in e-publishing. An excellent read for anyone interested in internet business.

Cybertrends: Chaos, Power and Accountability in the Information Age
David Brown
An interesting 'makes you think' book.

Digital Business: Surviving and Thriving in an On-Line World
Ray Hammond
Essential reading for e-business people.

How To Grow Your Business On The Internet
Vince Emery
A very American book, but with lots of useful information.

Infopreneurs: Online and Global
H. Skip Weitzen and Rick Parkhill
Excellent reading if you want to make money from selling information online.

Web Sites That Suck: Learn Good Design by Looking at Bad Design
Vincent Flanders and Michael Willis
An excellent book that every web-site owner should read.

Webonomics
Evan I. Schwartz
An interesting look at e-commerce and how to make money from it.

Glossary of internet terms

Address book – A **directory** in a web **browser** where you can store people's email addresses. This saves having to type them out each time you want to email someone.

AltaVista – A popular internet **search engine** used to find pages relating to specific keywords entered.

AOL – America Online, the world's biggest **internet service provider**, with more than ten million subscribers. It has given away hundreds of thousands of free CDs with the popular computer magazines to build its customer base.

Archie – Search system for looking for files.

Article – The name given to a message posted in a **newsgroup**. The term 'article' applies even if the message only runs to a couple of words.

ASCII – American Standard Code for Information Interchange. It is a simple text file format that can be accessed by most word processors and text editors. It is a universal file type for passing textual information across the internet.

Ask Jeeves – A popular internet **search engine**. Rather than just typing in a few key words for your search, you can type in a whole question or instruction, such as 'Find me everything about online marketing.'

Associate programme – Working with another site for mutual benefit.

Attachment – A file sent with an email message. The attached file may be a word-processed document, a database, spreadsheet, graphic or even a sound or video file. For example, you could email someone birthday greetings, and attach a sound track or photograph of yourself.
As a student, you could email your tutor and attach a file containing the text of your essay.

Automessaging – See **autoresponder**.

Autoresponder – Software that replies to a message automatically.

Bandwidth – The width of the electronic highway that gives you access to the internet. The higher the bandwidth, the wider this highway, and the faster the traffic can flow.

Banner ad – This is a band of text and graphics, usually situated at the top of a web page. A banner acts like a title, telling the user what the content of the page is about. It invites the visitor to click on it to visit that site.

Baud rate – The data transmission speed in a **modem**, measured in bps (bits per second).

BBS – Bulletin board service.

Bookmark – A file of **URL**s of your favourite internet sites. Bookmarks are very easily created by bookmarking (mouse-clicking) any internet page you like the look of.

Boolean search – A search in which you type in words such as AND and OR to refine your search. The words are called 'Boolean operators', after George Boole, a nineteenth-century English mathematician.

Brand – Heinz is a brand. Yours must become as well known as this in your sector for net success.

Browser – This is software that allows you to browse through internet pages and download useful information. Internet Explorer and Netscape Navigator are by far the most popular browsers available. Your **internet service provider** will normally supply a free browser when you sign up.

Bulletin board – A computer service that provides an email service and a file archive.

Cache – A file storage area on a computer. Your web browser will normally cache (copy to your hard drive) each web page you visit. When you revisit that page on the web, you may in fact be looking at the page originally cached on your computer. To be sure you are viewing the current page, press **reload** – or **refresh** – on your browser toolbar. You can empty your cache from time to time, and the computer will do so automatically whenever the cache is full.

Certificate – A computer file that identifies a personal or organisation on the internet.

Click through – This is when someone clicks on a **banner ad** or other **link**, for example, and is moved from that page to the advertiser's web site.

Client side – Your side of the host/client relationship between you and your **ISP**.

Closed areas – Areas of a web site that only registered users can enter.

Community – The internet is often described as a net community. This refers to the fact that many people enjoy belonging to a group of like-minded individuals.

Glossary ....

Company profile – This refers to details relating to the activities, performance and ethos of a company – useful for people looking to research a company's background.

Compression – Computer files can be electronically compressed, so that they can be uploaded or downloaded more quickly across the internet, saving time and money. If an image file is compressed too much, there may be a loss of quality.

Content – Articles, columns, sales messages, images and the text of your web site.

Content services – Web sites dedicated to a particular subject.

Crash – What happens when a computer program malfunctions. The operating system of your PC may perform incorrectly or come to a complete stop ('freeze'), forcing you to shut down and restart. A crash is more likely to happen when you have several windows and several software programs running simultaneously.

Cross-posting – Posting messages into several groups with the same text in each message.

Cyberspace – Popular term for the intangible 'place' where you go to surf; the ethereal world of computers and telecommunications on the internet.

Database marketing – Using data from databases to assist in marketing to specific customers or market segments.

Dial In Account – This allows you to connect your computer to your internet service provider's computer remotely.

Digital – Based on the binary digits 0 and 1. The operation of all computers is based on this fundamentally simple concept. All forms of information are capable of being digitalised – numbers, words, sounds and images.

Digital certificate – Means of authenticating yourself online.

Direct email – The online term for direct mailing.

Directory – On a PC, a folder containing your files.

Domain name – The domain name of an internet site identifies the organisation or computer hosting that internet site, followed by an identifier detailing the type of site. For example, lawcouncil.gov would probably be a government organisation called Law Council. A DNS (domain name server) translates the user-friendly domain name into the technical IP address.

Download – The term used to describe copying a file from the internet to your desktop PC or laptop. The opposite term – copying a file from your computer to one on the internet – is **upload**.

E-business – The broad concept of doing business-to-business and business-to-consumer sales over the internet.

E-commerce – The various means and techniques of transacting business online.

Email –   Short for electronic mail, a message sent across the internet to an individual or group of individuals.

Email address – The unique address given to you by your ISP. It can be used by others using the internet to send email messages to you. An example of a standard email address is:

mybusiness@aol.com

Emoticons – Popular symbols used to express emotions in email, for example:

:-) which means 'I'm smiling!'

Emoticons are not normally appropriate for business communications.

Excite – A popular internet **directory** and **search engine** used to find pages relating to specific **keywords** which you enter. See also **Yahoo!**.

E-zines – Magazines and newsletters which only exist on the internet.

FAQ – Short for Frequently Asked Questions. This refers to text files held in **newsgroups** and on internet pages that give answers to the most commonly asked questions people ask about the activity of the site. Always read FAQs before leaving any message relating to the problem that you are experiencing, or the question that you wish answered.

Favorites – The rather coy term for **bookmarks** used by **Internet Explorer**, and by **America Online**.

Field – Area such as the subject line in your **email**.

File – A file is a body of data such as a word-processed document, a spreadsheet, a database file, a graphics file or sound file.

Firewall – A firewall is special software designed to stop the flow of certain files into and out of a computer network.

Flame – A more or less hostile or aggressive message posted in a **newsgroup** or to an individual newsgroup user. If they get out of hand there can be flame wars.

Glossary ....

Folder – The name for a **directory** on a computer. It is a place in which files are stored.

Form – A means of collecting data on web pages, using text boxes and buttons.

Forums – These are similar to **usenet** groups and allow you to read, **post** and reply to messages.

Frames – A web design feature in which web pages can be divided into several areas, each containing separate information. A typical set of frames in a page includes an index frame (with navigation links), a banner frame (for a heading), and a body frame (for text matter).

Freebies – The 'give away' products, services or other enticements offered on a web site to attract registrations.

Freespace – The term for no-cost web space offered by internet access providers and others as an incentive to private and business users. The amount of freespace offered typically varies from 2 megabytes to 10 megabytes. Sometimes there are restrictions on the kind of material you can place in freespace.

Freeware – Software programs made available without charge. Where a small charge is requested, the term is **shareware**.

Front page – The first page of your web site that the visitor will see. FrontPage is also the name of a popular web-authoring package from **Microsoft**.

FTP – Short for file transfer protocol, the method normally used to send files back and forth across the internet. The term is a bit off-putting, but 'ftp-ing' is not difficult to do once you have some popular basic software, such as WS_FTP.

GIF – Short for graphic information file. It is a compressed file format used on the internet to display files that contain graphic images. See also **JPEG**.

Gopher – A text-based document search system.

GUI – Short for graphic user interface. It describes the friendly screens found in **Windows** and other WIMP environments (Windows, icons, mice, pointers).

Hacker – Someone who makes or seeks to make an unauthorised entry into someone else's computer system or network.

History list – A record of visited web pages. Your **browser** probably includes a history list. It is handy way of revisiting sites whose addresses you have forgotten to **bookmark** – just click on the item you want in the history list. You can normally delete all or part of the history list in your browser.

Hits – The number of times your web site has been visited.

Hit counter – Software that records your **hits**.

Home page – This refers to the index page of an individual or an organisation on the internet. It usually contains links to related pages of information and to other relevant sites.

Host computer – This is a computer that is directly connected to the internet. When you sign up with an **internet service provider** you have access to your ISP's computer, which then serves as the host computer for your access.

HotBot – This is a popular internet **search engine** used to find pages relating to any **keywords** you decide to enter. A 'bot' means a robot – in internet terms, a piece of software that performs a task on the internet, such as searching.

HTML – Short for hypertext mark-up language. It is a kind of word-processing language used by internet users to develop pages which can be uploaded and viewed across the internet using a **browser**. You write your text, and then use a universally accepted system of tags to indicate such things as type size, bold, italic, headings, colours and so on.

HTTP – Hyper text transfer protocol. It is the standard way that HTML documents are transferred from host computer to your local **browser** when you're surfing the internet. You'll see this acronym at the start of every web address, for example:

$$http://www.abcxyz.com$$

Hypertext – This is a link on an HTML page which, when clicked with a mouse, results in a further HTML page or graphic being loaded into view on your **browser**.

Information fatigue – The point at which people become tired of reading information and stop taking it in.

Infoseek – One of the leading internet **search engines**.

Internet – This is a broad term for the fast-expanding network of global computers that can access each other in a standard way. If you have a **modem** on your computer, you too are part of the internet. The term encompasses email, web pages, internet chat, newsgroups, gopher and telnet, rather as the term 'the printed word', for example, refers to books, magazines, newspapers, catalogues, leaflets and posters. The 'internet' does not exist in one place or under one authority any more than 'the printed word' does.

Glossary ....

Internet account – The account set up by your **internet service provider** which gives you access to the **world wide web**, **electronic mail** facilities, **newsgroups** and other value added services.

Internet Explorer – The world's most popular browser software, a product of **Microsoft** and keen rival to Netscape (recently taken over by **America Online**).

Internet service provider – ISPs are commercial, educational or official organisations which offer internet access to users. Commercial ISPs usually have a monthly fixed charge. Services typically include access to the **world wide web**, **electronic mail**, access to **newsgroups**, as well as a number of other services such as news, chat and entertainment.

Internic – Organisation that looks after domain names.

Intranet – A private computer network that uses internet technology to allow communication between individuals within, for example, a large commercial organisation. It often operates on a **LAN** (local area network).

IP address – An 'internet protocol' address. All computers linked to the internet have one. The address is somewhat like a telephone number, and consists of four sets of numbers separated by dots.

IRC – Internet relay chat. Chat is an enormously popular part of the internet, and there are all kinds of chat rooms and chat software. The chat involves typing messages which are sent and read in real time.

ISDN – Integrated Services Digital Network. A high-speed telephone network that can send computer data from the internet to your PC faster than a normal telephone line.

Java – An internet programming language developed by Sun Microsystems, used to improve the appearance and functioning features of web pages.

JPEG – The acronym is short for Joint Photographic Experts Group. A JPEG is a specialised file format used to display graphic files on the internet. JPEG files are smaller than similar **GIF** files and so have become ever more popular – even though there is sometimes a feeling that their quality is not as good as GIF format files. See also **MPEG**.

Keywords – Words that sum up your web site for being indexed in **search engines**. For example, for a cosmetics site the keywords might include beauty, lipstick, make-up, fashion, cosmetic and so on.

LAN – Local area network, a computer network usually located in one building.

Links – Small pieces of highlighted text or graphics that move you from one web site to another, or to another page within a web site. You activate the link by clicking it with your mouse. Text links are often underlined so you can see they are links.

Listserver – Software that runs a mailing list.

Living document – A document which is constantly evolving.

Log on/log off – To access/leave a network. In the early days of computing this literally involved making a record in a log book.

Lurk – The slang term used to describe reading a **newsgroup**'s messages without actually taking part in that newsgroup. Despite the connotations of the word, it is a perfectly respectable activity on the internet.

Mail server – A remote computer that enables you to send and receive emails. Your internet access provider will usually act as your mail server.

Mailing list – An electronic facility on the internet. You can subscribe to any number of mailing lists on the internet: there are thousands of them catering for every interest. Any new information that might be of interest to you is then downloaded to your PC automatically (for example, every day or every week). You can normally quit a mailing list by sending an email message to request removal. You can, of course, have your own conventional mailing list of customers.

Mall (or I-mall) – Shopping area online.

Marquee – Tool used in Microsoft FrontPage and other web-design packages. Also HTML 'tag' or code.

Merchant account – Allows you to use credit cards as payment.

Meta-tags – The technical term for the **keywords** used in your web page code to help search-engine software rank your site.

Microcash – One of the non-cash e-trade systems.

Microsoft – The big company behind the **Windows** operating system.

Modem – The word derives from MOdulator/DEModulator. This is an internal or external piece of hardware plugged into your PC. It links into a standard phone socket, thereby giving you access to the internet.

Moderator – A person in charge of a **mailing list**, **newsgroup** or **forum**. The moderator prevents unwanted messages.

MPEG – The file format used for video clips available on the internet. See also **JPEG**.

Glossary ....

Multi-phased medium – The internet is a multi-phased medium. That is, it can be used in many different ways to do many different things.

Navigate – To click on the hyperlinks on a web site in order to move to other web pages or internet sites.

Net – A slang term for the internet. In the same way, the world wide web is often just called the web.

Netiquette – Popular term for the unofficial rules and language used to keep electronic communication in an acceptably polite form.

Netscape – After **Internet Explorer**, Netscape is the most popular browser software available for surfing the internet. An excellent browser, Netscape has suffered in the wake of the rise of Microsoft's Internet Explorer, mainly because of the success of **Microsoft** in getting it installed on most new PCs. Netscape has recently been taken over by America Online for $4 billion.

Nettie – Someone who likes to spend a lot of time on the internet.

Newbie – Popular term for a new member of a **newsgroup** or **mailing list**.

News feed – Where your news comes from.

News reader – Software that enables you to search, read, post and manage messages in a newsgroup.

News server – A remote computer that enables you to access newsgroups.

Newsgroups – These form a special area of the internet ('**usenet**') where anyone can discuss things around a subject of common interest. The discussion takes the form of posting messages, which everyone in the newsgroup can then read. Posting and reading messages is much like sending and reading email. There are upwards of 30,000 active newsgroups on the internet.

Niche – Market segment. For example, you serve **SME**s in the database marketing sector.

Nominet – Internet domain name organisation.

Off-portalling – Reading web-site portals offline rather than online.

Online – The time you spend linked via a **modem** to the internet. You can keep your phone bill down by reducing online time. The opposite term is offline.

OS – The operating system in a computer, for example MS DOS (Microsoft Disk Operating System) or Windows 95/98.

PC – Personal computer.

Personalisation – Using information to 'personalise' an email or other material.

PoP – Point of Presence. This refers to the number of local-dial telephone numbers available from your ISP. If your ISP does not have a local access number or PoP, then don't sign up – your telephone bill will rocket. All the big ISPs have local numbers all over the UK.

Portal site – Portal means gateway. A portal site is one loaded into your web browser as soon as you connect to the internet. It could, for example, be the front page of your **internet service provider** such as AOL, Demon or Virgin Net; or you can set your browser to make it some other front page – for example, a **search engine** such as Yahoo!, or even your own front page.

Post – The common term used for sending ('posting') messages to a **newsgroup**. Posting messages is very like sending emails.

Protocol – Technical term for the method by which computers communicate.

Rank – Your place on the list of web sites produced by a **search engine**, as a result of someone doing a search.

Refresh, reload – Reload a web site page or site.

Registered user – Someone who has filled out an online form and then been granted special access to restricted areas of a web site. Access is then usually obtained by entering a password and user name.

Search engine – A piece of software that allows you to access information by typing in any key words of your choice. There are lots of free search engines on the internet - Yahoo!, AltaVista, Infoseek, Excite, Ask Jeeves, Lycos and Webcrawler to name but a few. Many bigger web sites have their own search engines to help you find what you are looking for on their sites.

Secure servers – The hardware and software provided so that people can use their credit cards and leave other details without the risk of others seeing them online.

Secure sockets layer (SSL) – This allows credit-card transactions to be done securely.

Secure transactions – A safe way of doing credit-card transactions.

Server – Any computer on a network that provides access and serves information to other computers.

Shareware – Software which, although free, comes with a moral obligation to send a small donation to the author should you continue use of the software after a trial period (usually between 30 and 90 days). A vast amount of shareware is now available on the internet.

Signature file – This is a computer file in which you can place your address details and which you can add to email and newsgroup messages. You only need to create a signature file once and you can then append it to your emails as often as you like.

Site maintenance – Keeping your site up to date on a regular basis.

Smiley – A form of **emoticon**.

Spam – The popular term for electronic junk mail – unsolicited and unwelcome email messages sent across the internet. There are various forms of spam-busting software which you can now obtain to filter out unwanted messages.

Special interest groups – Rather like **newsgroups** and **forums**, 'special interest groups' are areas where people interested in a certain subject can meet online.

Snail mail – Popular term for the standard postal service involving post-persons, vans, trains, planes, sacks and sorting offices.

Strategic alliance – A partnership between two businesses serving the same customers with different products.

Subscribe – Term for accessing a **newsgroup** in order to read and post messages in the newsgroup. There is no charge, and you can subscribe, unsubscribe and resubscribe at any time at the click of your mouse.

Surfing – The act of browsing the internet, especially following trails of links on pages on the world wide web.

Sysop – Systems operator, someone rather like a **moderator**.

TCP/IP – Transmission Control Protocol/Internet Protocol, the essential technology of the internet. It's not normally something you need worry about.

Telnet – Software that allows you to connect via the internet to a remote computer and work as if you were a terminal linked to that system.

Theme – A term in web-page design. A theme describes the general colours and graphics used within a web site. Many themes are available in the form of ready-made templates.

Thread – An ongoing topic in a **usenet newsgroup** or **mailing list** discussion. The term refers to the original message on a particular topic, and all the replies and other messages which spin off from it. With news-reading software you can easily 'view thread' and read these messages in a convenient batch.

Traffic – The number of people visiting your site.

Under construction – A site which is still being built.

UNIX – This is an operating system that has been in use for many years and is still used in many larger systems. Most ISPs use this operating system.

Unmoderated – A mailing list or group which does not have a **moderator**.

Uploading – The act of copying files from your **PC** to a server or other PC on the internet (for example, when you are publishing your own web pages). The term is most commonly used to describe the act of copying **HTML** pages onto the internet via **FTP**.

URL – Uniform resource locator. In plain English, it means the full address of a particular **world wide web** page, for example:

http://www.internet-handbooks.co.uk

USP – Unique sales point, a vital marketing requirement for any product or service.

Usenet – A large area of the internet consisting of more than 30,000 special interest **newsgroups** on many different subjects. People can read messages left by others and send or post their own. Each set of messages on a particular subject within a group is called a **thread**.

Veronica – Another text-based search facility.

Virus – A piece of software which attacks your software.

Virtual reality – Computer-generated simulations.

Visitors – The people who come to your web site, the source of your **hits**.

Wallet – Tool in **Internet Explorer** for online transactions.

Web authoring – Creating **HTML** pages to upload onto the internet. You will be a web author if you create your own home page for uploading onto the internet.

Webcrawler – A popular internet **search engine** used to find pages relating to specific **keywords** entered.

Glossary ....

Webmaster – Person in charge of a web site.

Web pages – The images and text you see in your browser window.

Web rings – Collections of web sites and pages.

Web site – A collection of web pages.

Windows – The ubiquitous operating system for personal computers, developed by the Microsoft Corporation. The Windows 3.1 version was followed by Windows 95 and, most recently, Windows 98.

World wide web – Or 'web' for short. The most popular element of the internet, made up of tens of millions of web pages, usually containing text, images, hyperlinks, sounds and even video clips.

WYSIWYG – 'What you see is what you get.' If you see it on the screen, then it should look just the same when you print it out.

Yahoo! – Probably the world's most popular internet **directory** and **search engine**.

Zip/unzip – Many files that you download from the internet will be in compressed format, especially if they are large files. This makes them quicker to download. These files are said to be zipped or compressed. Unzipping these compressed files generally refers to the process of returning them to their original size on receipt. Zip files have the extension '.zip' and are created using WinZip software or a similar package.

Index

Index ....